PARAGONE

A COMPARISON OF THE ARTS

A female head

PARAGONE

A COMPARISON OF THE ARTS BY
LEONARDO DA VINCI

WITH AN INTRODUCTION AND
ENGLISH TRANSLATION
BY
IRMA A. RICHTER

GEOFFREY CUMBERLEGE
OXFORD UNIVERSITY PRESS
LONDON   NEW YORK   TORONTO
MCMXLIX

Oxford University Press, Amen House, London E.C. 4

GLASGOW NEW YORK TORONTO MELBOURNE WELLINGTON
BOMBAY CALCUTTA MADRAS CAPE TOWN

Geoffrey Cumberlege, Publisher to the University

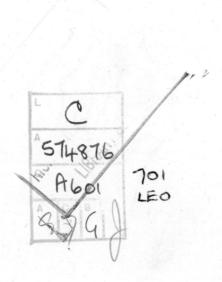
PRINTED IN GREAT BRITAIN
AT THE UNIVERSITY PRESS, OXFORD
BY CHARLES BATEY, PRINTER TO THE UNIVERSITY

PREFACE

PARAGONE, or 'comparison of the arts', is the modern title given to the first chapter of a treatise on painting by Leonardo da Vinci, which is now in the Vatican Library and formerly belonged to the Ducal Library at Urbino.[1] It is not a connected literary treatise, but is made up of notes copied from the original manuscripts of the master and dovetailed together. The editor may have been Francesco Melzi, his pupil and friend.

Since most of Leonardo's own manuscripts quoted in this first chapter are no longer extant, Dr. J. P. Richter decided to include it in the second edition of the *Literary Works of Leonardo da Vinci* (1939), which otherwise reproduces only texts in the Master's own handwriting. Its translation and the introductory essays thereto were my contribution to my father's work, which has now again gone out of print; and since there is no other English version extant, the Oxford University Press has agreed to publish it with the Italian text in a separate volume.

The Paragone forms an important contribution to the literature on the comparison of the arts. The discussion, which in Leonardo's time was prompted by a rivalry among artists, foreshadows the beginning of comparative criticism. It was taken up by other artists and led to the questionnaire sent out by Benedetto Varchi in 1546 to Florentine painters and sculptors. Pontormo's and Michelangelo's replies are reproduced in this volume and will give a picture of this controversy between artists about their crafts. Venice took up the cause of painting against the Florentine sculptors. The discussion was pursued in the following centuries by theorists and academicians in Italy and France. It eventually developed into an investigation of the possibilities and limitations of the various arts and their media. Leonardo's question 'Which is the better art' became an inquiry as to 'which art is better in respect to what'; and was answered in Lessing's *Laokoon* in a way that Leonardo had forecast.

A way was being prepared for aesthetics as an independent branch of philosophy. But the Paragone is also of interest because it reveals the views of a leading artist of the Renaissance about art. It reflects his pride

---

[1] Trattato della Pittura, Codex Vaticanus (Urbinas), 1270. The title 'Paragone' was first used in G. Manzi's edition of the treatise, Rome, 1817.

and self-assurance as he approaches every subject with reliance on his own experience and initiative. His universality and his manifold activities in mathematics, in natural sciences, in mechanics, engineering, in music, in painting, sculpture, and architecture make him a representative spokesman of the arts and sciences such as our age of specialization no longer produces. His mind was able to grasp the unity of all the arts.

But his age was not ripe for precise scientific analysis; and his arguments naturally had to take into account the ideas on art prevalent at his time which were shrouded in scholastic and humanist preconceptions. Art criticism, as we understand it, did not exist, and the criteria by which poetry was judged were not literary criteria. We may often be more concerned with the implications than with the main theme, which may seem to be of no consequence to the modern reader. At other times he expresses thoughts that were not developed till centuries later and are still valid to-day. For the comparison of the arts continues. It is still far the best means by which an understanding of the methods and resources of any one of them can be attained; and while we are now more discriminating than in the past, when one art was often made to legislate for another, Leonardo's Paragone may be said to have started us on our quest.

The art of the Renaissance forms part of our European heritage. The motives that inspired it are both temporal and timeless; and we may appreciate their significance if we compare and contrast them with what came before and after.

In the Introduction I have therefore briefly described the views about art and their sources in Leonardo's time, and I have also compared his own views with those of later generations and with certain modern concepts. But in giving his views I had to aline them into a consecutive argument. For, as stated above, his treatise is but a collection of excerpts taken from different manuscripts; relevant passages were copied and sometimes added outside their context; and since he was apt to repeat himself in his notes, numerous repetitions have crept into the compilation. It was evidently impossible for the editor to knit the material together in logical sequence in this preliminary draft.

To Professor Erwin Panofsky, Professor Rensselaer Lee, and Professor Frank J. Mather I am indebted for encouragement in the writing of this book.

The copyright of such illustrations as are based upon drawings in

the Windsor Collection is vested in his Majesty the King, and I take this opportunity of expressing my deep sense of gratitude for the facilities which I have been granted in this matter. I wish to thank the authorities of the Institut de France for allowing me to reproduce drawings in their keeping. The Albertina permitted the reproduction of their photograph of a drawing belonging to the Museum at Budapest. Other drawings here reproduced belong to the Louvre and to the Library at Turin to whom I am indebted.

To the Oxford University Press I owe thanks for permitting the reprint from their edition of J. P. Richter's *Literary Works of Leonardo da Vinci* and for their help in preparing this edition.

I. A. RICHTER

CONTENTS

I

PAINTING AND SCIENCE

[1] References to Ludwig's edition.

II

POETRY AND PAINTING

III

PAINTING, POETRY, AND MUSIC

IV

PAINTING AND SCULPTURE

LIST OF ILLUSTRATIONS

INTRODUCTION

CODEX URBINAS 1270[1]

THERE are several manuscripts extant of the sixteenth and seventeenth centuries purporting to be treatises of painting by Leonardo da Vinci. The oldest of these, and the only one that contains the *Paragone*, is preserved in the Vatican Library (Urbinas 1270). It is a compilation made from Leonardo's original manuscripts entitled 'Libro di Pittura di M. Leonardo da Vinci, Pittore et Scultore Fiorentino'. This codex was in the library of the Dukes of Urbino among the books collected by Francesco Maria della Rovere, the last Duke (d. 1631). The library passed into the possession of the popes in 1657 and was transferred then to the Vatican. There is no record of the previous history of the manuscript, when and under what circumstances it was compiled, and how it came to the ducal library; but from internal evidence we may infer that it was an attempt soon after Leonardo's death to make a selection from his various manuscripts preparatory to a publication. The book, 15 by 21 cm. in size, is bound in vellum and contains 331 numbered sheets. The illustrations accompanying the text were first lightly sketched in pencil and then drawn over in ink. The calligraphy is clear and regular and may be dated approximately in the sixteenth century. To judge by his language, the scribe was a Lombard. His spelling and punctuation were defective; and his work was supervised, for there are corrections in two other handwritings. That the copyist had Leonardo's original manuscripts before him is shown by his mention of the left-handed writing as an excuse for errors committed, and by the list at the end of his work of eighteen of these manuscripts from which he had copied sections. Of the total of 944 transcribed paragraphs in the compilation a few are still extant in the Master's own writing; the majority, however, are not to be found in the manuscripts that have survived. The compilation must therefore have been made when the collection of manuscripts which Leonardo left at his death was still more or less intact, as was the case when in the safe keeping of Francesco Melzi, who had inherited all Leonardo's literary remains and treasured them as his most precious possessions,

[1] Standard edition by H. Ludwig, Vienna, 1882.

keeping them like relics at his villa at Vaprio near Milan. But after his death in 1570 his son suffered the collection to be dispersed and by 1590 he had disposed of all the Master's writings. After that date so great a number of original manuscripts by Leonardo was never again assembled at one place.

The Codex Urbinas was therefore probably written while Leonardo's bequest was still with Francesco Melzi. He may, indeed, have been responsible for the compilation since his name is inscribed on three of its pages which were left blank as if reserved for his own use. The compilers seem to have proceeded tentatively and their work was open to revision. But, although left unpublished at that time, the Codex Urbinas 1270 became the source from which later copyists drew either directly or indirectly, and a book based on it was eventually published in Paris in 1651, in abbreviated form and without its first chapter, 'the Paragone'.[1]

---

[1] *Trattato della Pittura di Leonardo da Vinci novamente dato in luce con la vita dell' istesso autore scritta da Raffaelle Du Fresne,* Paris, 1651. For the history of Leonardo's treatise on painting see J. P. and I. A. Richter, *The Literary Works of Leonardo da Vinci,* second edition, 1939, vol. i, pp. 5–11.

NOTE

The texts of the *Paragone* have been arranged under four headings: I. Painting and Science; II. Painting and Poetry; III. Painting, Poetry, and Music; IV. Painting and Sculpture. They are only approximately in the sequence of the original manuscript which was but a first tentative arrangement.

References to Ludwig's standard edition of the Codex Urbinas 1270 are preceded by the letters 'Trat.' for (Trattato), while references to the original manuscripts published in J. P. Richter's *Literary Works of Leonardo da Vinci*, 1939, are preceded by the letter R. (for Richter).

LEONARDO ARTIST AND SCIENTIST

It is doubtful whether Leonardo intended his notes on the comparison of the arts for an introduction to his treatise on painting. The passages were probably selected and co-ordinated for this purpose by the compiler of the Codex Urbinas 1270, who very rightly considered them a suitable beginning. The style is animated and occasionally contains exaggerations such as might occur in debates. The wording sometimes assumes the form of an argumentative conversation between the representatives of the arts, and it has been suggested that these texts were originally memoranda for a debate such as Fra Luca Pacioli describes as taking place at the court of Milan between distinguished representatives of the arts and sciences (dedication of *De Divina Proportione*). Such dialogues were much favoured at the time, following their great prototypes, in classical literature, the advantage being that each point of view could be in turn clearly stated and controverted.

The court of Milan was a centre much frequented by poets and musicians. Duke Lodovico Sforza was glorified as the true Messiah of Italy and his city was compared to Athens in the time of her glory by Bernardo Bellincioni, the Florentine poet at his court. The Duchess Beatrice, sister of Isabella d'Este, loved poetry and music; and never a month passed without some new eclogue, comedy, tragedy, or some spectacle or play being performed, besides frequent recitations of poems. She organized a choir of her own which accompanied her on her journeys.

The arts were dependent on the patronage of rulers and of the Church, who determined their subject-matter. While Leonardo was painting the 'Virgin of the Rocks' and the 'Last Supper', he was also working on the equestrian monument of the Duke's father. As an architect he made designs for domes of churches and for a pavilion in the Duchess's garden. He took part in the activities at the court. His biographer Paolo Giovio[1] relates that he sang beautifully to his own accompaniment to the delight of the entire court. He designed costumes and sceneries for plays; he painted portraits; and, as stated above, he joined in debates about the arts. If we may think of him as holding forth in defence of his favourite art, we should bear in mind Vasari's description that with his arguments he silenced the learned, confounded

---

[1] See Index and R. Vol. I, pp. 1 and 2.

the liveliest intellect, and turned every long-established view. His powers of conversation were such as to draw to himself the souls of his listeners. In speaking he accompanied his words with persuasive gestures. Benvenuto Cellini was told in France soon after Leonardo's death that Francis I derived such pleasure from listening to him that he only parted from him for a few days of the year.

Let us briefly review his knowledge and experience in science, painting, music, sculpture, and poetry, the subjects under discussion in the *Paragone*. In a letter addressed to Lodovico Sforza he gives an account of his qualifications. He offers his services in war-time as a military engineer, and is ready to construct portable bridges, mortars, guns, indestructible chariots, and ships—'in short I can contrive various and endless means of offence and defence'.

'In time of peace I believe I can give perfect satisfaction and to the equal of any other in architecture and the composition of buildings public and private, and in guiding water from one place to another. I can carry out sculpture in marble, bronze or clay and also do in painting whatever may be done, as well as any other, be he who he may.

'Again the bronze horse may be taken in hand, which is to be to the immortal glory and eternal honour of the prince, your father of happy memory, and of the illustrious house of Sforza.' (R. 1340.)

The fact that he excelled in the arts of painting and sculpture is added at the end of Leonardo's letter. The stress is laid on his scientific qualifications as an engineer. But the real reason why he wrote it may have been his wish to secure the commission for the Sforza monument, as revealed in the last paragraph.

He felt competent to do so.[1] He had for years been studying as pupil and assistant in the studio of one of the most distinguished Florentine sculptors, Andrea Verrocchio, who was also a painter. His offer to serve as an engineer reveals his competence in another field. But his many-sided activities were all based on the study of the laws of nature and on mathematics. From the time of his boyhood, when he confounded his master by his questions, he was keenly interested in arithmetic. He often quoted Euclid. He excelled in geometry and drew the

---

[1] Baldassare Taccone, poet and chancellor at the Sforza court, for one of whose plays Leonardo designed the stage scenery, greatly admired the equestrian model as it stood unfinished in the court of the Castello at Milan, and in a poem compares the artist to Phidias, Myron, Scopas, and Praxiteles. See R., vol. i, p. 45.

illustrations for Fra Luca Pacioli's *De Divina Proportione*, which was based on the Thirteenth Book of Euclid's *Elements*. He was acquainted with Vitruvius' scheme of proportions of the human figure, and one of his drawings[1] served as an illustration in Fra Giocondo's edition of *De Architectura*, which appeared in Venice in 1511. As was his wont, he did not rely on the findings of others, but took measurements himself. He studied perspective by observation and experiment apart from any literature or information that may have been at his disposal. He was aware that linear perspective was a convention, which took for granted that vision was one-eyed, and which conceived of the organ of sight as a precise mathematical instrument in accordance with the ancient tradition that optics was a purely mathematical science, a branch of geometry; and he knew how to distinguish between the physiological aspect and these mathematical hypotheses. He examined the structure of the eye and its function, and in so doing perhaps discovered the natural phenomenon of the camera obscura.

His treatment of the subject-matter of painting was based on scientific research, pursued far beyond what would seem necessary for the application of his art. His anatomical and physiological studies induced him to dissect corpses. He wrote on the movement of the human figure, on questions of weight, balance, leverage, and centres of gravity. He planned to write a book on mechanics and designed all kinds of mechanical appliances. A note-book on the flight of birds, charmingly illustrated, reveals his keen interest in a subject which induced him to design aeroplanes.

The backgrounds of his pictures necessitated the study of landscapes, clouds, horizons, the growth of plants, the currents and reflections in water, the composition of rocks. He tried to trace the geological history of the earth from observations of fossils in mountain valleys. In order to satisfy his curiosity in astronomy he constructed magnifying-glasses.

His note-books are filled with memoranda on a great variety of subjects, and reveal a keen love for nature, an insatiable curiosity, and an indefatigable spirit of research.

The course of study which he intended that an artist should follow was extensive and profound. In a general introduction to his notes on anatomy he warns art students of the many difficulties and incidentally

[1] R., Plate XVIII.

PLATE II

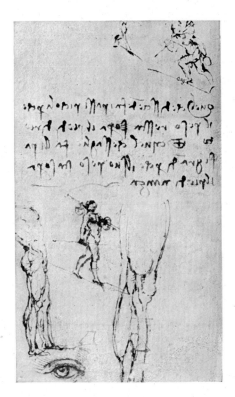

Drawings illustrating movements of the human figure

throws light on his own struggle. Referring to the dissection of corpses, he says:

'And if you should have a love for such things you might be prevented by loathing, and if that did not prevent you, you might be deterred by the fear of living in the night hours in the company of those corpses, quartered and flayed and horrible to see. And if this did not prevent you, perhaps you might not be able to draw so well as is necessary for such a demonstration; or if you had the skill of drawing, it might not be combined with knowledge of perspective; and if it were so, you might not understand the methods of geometrical demonstration and the method of the calculation of the forces and of the strength of the muscles. Patience may be wanting, so that you lack perseverance. As to whether all these things were found in me or not the hundred and twenty books (note-books) composed by me will give verdict Yes or No. In these I have been hindered neither by avarice nor negligence, but simply by want of time. Farewell!' (R. 796.)

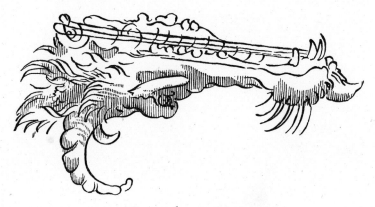

a. Leonardo as a Musician

Leonardo excelled also in music. In his youth he was resolved to acquire the art of playing the lyre, a guitar-shaped, bowed instrument, the predecessor of the violin. According to Vasari it was his accomplishment in music that was the cause of his summons to Milan by Lodovico Sforza; and on his arrival he is said to have won great applause in an assembly of musicians with a lyre which he had made himself largely of silver in the shape of a horse's skull, a new bizarre instrument producing a sound of great volume and clearness.

With the exception of the organ, the musical instruments of that time were mainly products of popular ingenuity. They were used to accompany voices; and their shapes were not as well defined as they are to-day.

But their construction began to engage the serious attention of thought-
ful musicians. It was a period of transition when foundations were laid
for the next important development of the art. Experiments were being
made with voices and instruments differing in pitch to achieve chord
effects, which involve some recognition of true harmony.

Leonardo took part in these experiments. When he says that it is the
harmony produced by the simultaneousness of the voices which makes
music like painting, he stresses an element in contemporary music which
contained the germs of modern musical art (p. 79, Trat. 32).

In his manuscripts we find drawings and notes dealing with the construction of musical instruments. On one sheet, amid calculations on the
sizes of organ-pipes the reader is referred to his book on the subject, now
lost (R. 7b). Another book 'De Vocie' (R. 7a), which is also lost,
treated of the human voice, 'that most sensitive of musical instruments'
(p. 76, Trat. 31). Among his anatomical notes we find detailed studies
of the organs that produce the voice—the mouth, the tongue, the
throat, the windpipe, which he compared to an organ-pipe.

He inquired into the physical aspect of sound, its echo, the cause of the
resonance of bells. He made plans for a church that would conform to
the requirements of acoustics. Like Vitruvius, he compared the vibration
of sound-waves to the circular waves caused by stones thrown on the
surface of a sheet of water; and observed that the water, although
remaining stationary, is stirred into sets of ever-widening circles, which
meet and cross, each retaining its course undisturbed. Centuries later
Helmholtz used the same simile to illustrate the passage of different
sound-waves through the same expanse of air without interference with
one another, while the human ear is able to distinguish between them
(R. 1130A).

Thus Leonardo applied his scientific methods of research also to
music. It is evident from his notes that he knew Boethius' treatise on
ancient music, but we have no definite information as to what other
works he may have read. He must have had frequent intercourse with
musicians. He liked to paint to the accompaniment of music. Vasari
relates that Mona Lisa was entertained by music during her sittings;
and he himself tells us that the sculptor is at a disadvantage because the
noise of the blows of his mallet precludes his listening to music while
at work (p. 95, Trat. 36). His first journey to Milan was made in the
company of the young Atalante Migliorotti, who later became renowned

PLATE III

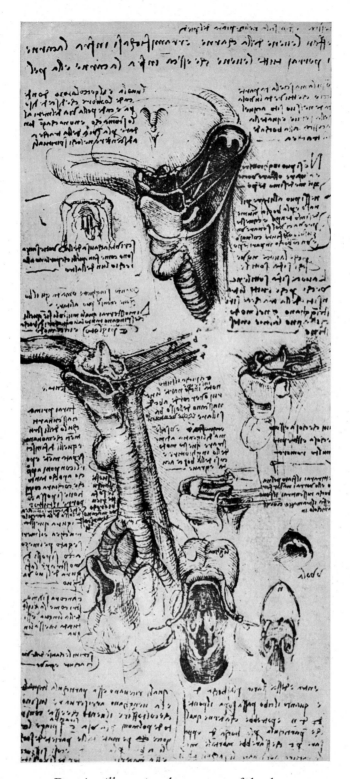

Drawing illustrating the anatomy of the throat

PLATE IV

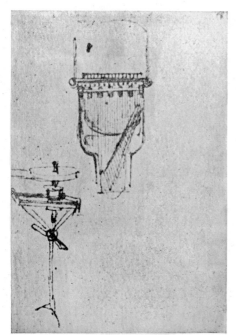

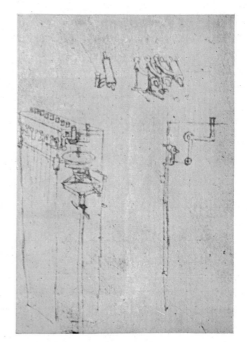

Three drawings illustrating musical instruments

as a maker of musical instruments. At the court and at the cathedral of Milan he had opportunities of meeting distinguished musicians. Franchino Gafori,[1] who was at the head of the far-famed cathedral choir, wrote a book on the theory of music which appeared in 1496. Though his art was still dominated by the medieval conceptions of descant, he affirmed in the last chapters that it is not enough for a composer to attend to the melodies of the parts, he must also combine them in a beautiful fusion of sound.[2]

b. Leonardo as a Writer

Leonardo could therefore be called expert in four of the five subjects that are under discussion in the *Paragone*. He was a scientist, a painter, a sculptor, and a musician. His knowledge of the art of poetry, on the other hand, was not based on his own experience. No writings in metrical form are extant which can with certainty be ascribed to him. But Lomazzo calls him a very amiable poet, 'un gentilissimo poeta' (*Idea del Tempio della Pittura*), and Vasari relates that he improvised songs, 'Cantò divinamente al improviso.'

Judging from his manuscripts he may with justice be called master of a language subtle, precise, and elevated, well adapted to express his thoughts. An eminent French writer in describing his style says: 'La belle idée que Léonard exprimait avec sa manière d'une spiritualité si mystérieuse' (M. Barrès, *Le Testament de Delacroix*). But his diction was that of the Florentine people. 'I am fully conscious that, not being a literary man, certain presumptuous persons think that they may blame me alleging that I am not a man of letters. . . . They do not know that my subjects are to be dealt with by experience rather than by words, and experience has been the mistress of those who write well'[3] (R. 10).

The study of classical literature, which was stirring the poets and men of letters of his time with a passion for learning and a craving for literary style, lay somewhat outside the scope of his genius. But the long lists of Latin and Italian words in some of Leonardo's note-books suggest that he may have felt the need of improving his vocabulary.

---

[1] A portrait supposed to represent him and attributed to Leonardo is at the Ambrosiana.

[2] Compare p. 72.

[3] A protest against such servile imitation of the classics as suggested by M. G. Vida for instance:

'Hence on ancients we must rest alone,
And make their golden sentences our own;
To cull their best expressions claims our cares,
To form our notions and our styles on theirs.'
(Trans. by C. Pitt.)

Benvenuto Cellini ascribed to Leonardo some knowledge of Latin and Greek literature; and judging from his manuscripts he was acquainted with parts of the works of Virgil, Horace, Ovid, Livy, and Pliny translated into the vulgar tongue. In one of his 'Prophecies' he deems those happy 'who lend ear to the words of the dead, who read good works and obey them' (R. 1300). In a list of his books (R. 1469), which includes almost every branch of contemporary learning, the following poetical works are mentioned: Luigi Pulci's *Morgante*, Lucio Pulci's *Driadeo*, Burchiello's *Sonnets*, *Il Manganello*, Frezzi's *Quadriregio*, Cecco d'Ascoli's *Acerba*, Goro Dati's *Spera*, *Petrarca*. He preferred Dante to Petrarch, about whose coronation on the Capitol he made a satirical comment (R. 1332), and in his manuscripts we find quotations from the *Inferno* (R. 965A) and from the *Convivio* (R. 10. 1479).

He made a number of transcriptions (R. 1220–34, 1264) from an Italian Bestiary entitled *Fior di Virtù* (1488), in which animals real or fabulous are described in the manner of natural history and deliberately

presented as a type of Christian life or doctrine. This kind of allegory appealed to him. *Aesop's Fables* were among his books, and he composed a number of fables himself (R. 1265–79) founded on observations of animals, plants, and natural phenomena. These ingenious little stories and jests afford interesting glimpses into his outlook on daily life. The same may be said of his 'Prophecies' (R. 1293–1310). His finest writing, however, was composed when he was carried away by enthusiasm for his art; when, for instance, he tried to prove that painting was greater than poetry.

Leonardo's estimate of poets as voiced in the *Paragone* must have been influenced by the poets whom he met at the court in Milan, whose business it was to write in support of the policies of their patrons, in celebration of their birthdays and weddings. Renaissance princes considered poets the necessary adornment of their court, for by them their guests were entertained and their names glorified. The time of Dante had passed when poets felt called upon as apostles of truth to sacrifice home and comforts for an ideal. The historian Benedetto Varchi

describes the poetry of this time as having gone from bad to worse ever since the death of Petrarch, until it was almost irrecognizable (Ercolano, 1560, p. 58). A leading burlesque writer, Francesco Berni (1498–1535), taunts the poets in his amusing *Dialogo contro i poeti* for their vanity and obsequiousness and for the degradation of their art. The decadence was no doubt also partly due to a lack of appreciation of the deeper implications of classical art, which they tried to imitate by the adoption of allegorical and mythological subjects and by a display of classical learning.

Among the numerous poets that flocked to the court of Milan was Bernardo Bellincioni.[1] A Florentine by birth, he had come well versed in the art of flattery from the courts of Lorenzo il Magnifico and Lodovico Gonzaga. A performance that contributed to his fame was the festival at the University of Pavia which was attended by Duke Lodovico and his Duchess and by the Duke of Ferrara and Isabella d'Este as their guests. Personifications of the Liberal Arts and of the Four Elements appeared singing side by side with Juno and Mercury, while the author recited stanzas in glorification of his illustrious audience. He collaborated with Leonardo in the 'Festa del Paradiso', given on the 13th of January 1490 for the entertainment of Gian Galeazzo Sforza and his young bride at the Castello of Milan. An enormous gilt hemisphere with the signs of the Zodiac was put on the stage; and the Planets, personified by the Greek Gods, recited stanzas in honour of the young wife.

Leonardo's arguments show that he was well versed in the aspirations of the poets of his time, though not a poet himself. He spontaneously acknowledged Michelangelo's superiority in this field. While discussing a passage from Dante with friends on the Piazza Santa Trinità in Florence, he saw his great rival pass by and immediately turned to him for an interpretation.[2]

[1] The small copper engraving in the collection of Edmond de Rothschild in the Louvre representing Bellincioni sitting at his desk was probably made after a drawing by Leonardo. A woodcut of the same portrait served as frontispiece to the 1493 edition of Bellincioni's *Rime*. Compare P. Kristeller, *Lombardische Graphik*, p. 20.

[2] For an account of the incident and of Michelangelo's rebuff see *Anonymus Magliabechianus*, ed. Frey, p. 115,

THE STATUS OF THE ARTS IN ANTIQUITY AND IN THE MIDDLE AGES

'Paragone', that is, comparison, rivalry of the Liberal Arts among themselves and with other arts that were excluded from their number. This was Leonardo's theme in the introductory chapter to the *Trattato della Pittura*. It can only be understood and appreciated if we make ourselves acquainted with the conceptions about art prevalent at his time. The Liberal Arts were so named because they were considered fit occupations for free-born citizens, and nobler than the labour of handicraftsmen or slaves. This distinction may be traced back to Plato, who appraised the arts according to their conduciveness towards good citizenship in his *Republic*. Somewhat later Latin writers classified them systematically under seven headings: Grammar, Dialectic, and Rhetoric represented the rational side dealing with language and logic; Arithmetic, Geometry, Astronomy, and Music represented the scientific side and were based on mathematics. Both groups served as *disciplines* or instruments of knowledge; and between them they formed the foundation of higher education. Such English phrases as Bachelor of Arts, Master of Arts recall this ancient conception.

In these lists we look in vain for the arts of painting and sculpture.[1] They were classed among the Mechanical Arts, which required manual labour and craftsmanship.[2] Still, Painting was sometimes practised by persons of distinction, and accepted by some classical writers as a preliminary step towards a 'liberal' education (Aristotle, *Politics*, viii. 1338 a; Pliny, *H.N.* xxxv. 76–7). It was often compared to Poetry which was related to Rhetoric and therefore connected with the Liberal Arts. But Sculpture had no such distinguished connexions.

Lucian's account of the position of the sculptor is described in his apologue 'The Vision'. Two women appeared to him in a dream after he had spent a disagreeable day as apprentice in the workshop of a sculptor. 'One of the women seemed a working woman, masculine looking, with untidy hair, horny hands, and dress kilted up; she was powdered with plaster'—this was Statuary;[3] 'The other woman had a

---

[1] For an account of the status of the Fine Arts and artists in Greece see Bernhard Schweitzer, *Der bildende Künstler und der Begriff des Künstlerischen in der Antike*, 1925; and Gisela M. A. Richter, *The Sculpture and Sculptors of the Greeks*, 1925, pp. 159 ff.

[2] Compare p. 25, Trat. 33.

[3] Compare p. 95, Trat. 36.

beautiful face, comely figure and neat attire'—and she was Culture, who said: 'The advantages that the profession of a sculptor will bring with it amount to no more than being a worker with four hands. . . . You will be just a worker, one of the masses cowering before the distinguished. . . . You may turn out a Phidias or a Polykleitos, to be sure, and create a number of wonderful works, but you will always rank as a common craftsman who makes his living with his hands.'

Such casual references in classical literature naturally give but an incomplete picture of the status of the arts in antiquity. We must remember, for instance, that Pericles was a great friend of Phidias. The conception that art was creative had its supporters, and is reflected in the Hymn to Zeus by Kleanthes, where God appears as the *artifex mundi* wielding the thunderbolt as a chisel.

With the growth of Christianity the arts as classified by the Romans were incorporated in the Christian doctrine and became an integral part of the scholastic system.[1] Their division and relative importance within a comprehensive order embracing all human knowledge and experience were a source of infinite discussion during the Middle Ages. The *Artes Liberales* were looked upon as *disciplinae* whereby man could conquer the ignorance, which had descended upon him at the Fall, and the exiled soul return to wisdom. Here Painting was allowed to help save the uneducated. Gregory the Great wrote: 'Painting is admissible in churches in order that those who are unlettered may yet see by gazing at the walls what they cannot read in books.'[2] Our 'Fine Arts' were in the Middle Ages close neighbours to all kinds of crafts. They were classed with the *Artes Mechanicae*, which involved manual labour and served to deliver mankind from bodily needs. Architects and sculptors were also masons. Artists and craftsmen were organized in guilds, and were socially on an equal footing.

One of the last writers to restate the scholastic classification of the arts and sciences was Leonardo's contemporary Girolamo Savonarola. In a pamphlet entitled *De Divisione et Utilitate Omnium Scientiarum*, written in about 1492 in answer to an accusation that he despised poetry, he drew up a table assigning to each subject its proper position and rank. In order to show his appreciation of Poetry he gave her the place

---

[1] For an account of the classification of arts and sciences in the Middle Ages see Dr. Baur, *Dominicus Gundissalinus, De Divisione Philosophiae*, 1903.
[2] Roger Hinks, *Carolingian Art*, p. 97.

of Grammar as a member of the Liberal Arts. In all other respects this
table is fundamentally the same as that endorsed by previous scholastic
writers and shows the relationships between the sciences and arts in
systematic form. Philosophy, which meant the Theology of Scholasti-
cism, heads the list, and below it are ranged the human activities whereby
man could contribute towards his own salvation. Theology is the true
and only science; all others treat of special things under special aspects,
Theology alone treats of all under a single aspect. Theology is the first
science tracing all things to the first cause.

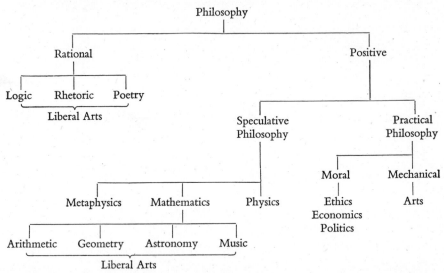

Thus in Leonardo's lifetime the scholastic case was stated once more
by a follower of St. Thomas Aquinas—just as the tide was rising that
was to sweep away the whole system.

a. Leonardo's Challenge

'Leonardo . . . has added great lustre to the art of painting. He laid down that all proper practice
of the art should be preceded by a training in the Sciences and Liberal Arts, which he regarded
as indispensable and subservient to painting.'—PAOLO GIOVIO.

In claiming a place for Painting among the Liberal Arts Leonardo
was challenging a long-established system which had been popularized
by writers and painters.[1] He accepted the principles on which it was

[1] For instance, one of the frescoes painted
by Botticelli on the walls of the Villa Lemmi
in 1486, to celebrate the marriage of Lorenzo
Tornabuoni with Giovanna degli Albizzi, represented the bridegroom being introduced
by Minerva to the seven graceful maidens
seated on their thrones. Compare pp. 11, 15.

based, but wished to see it amended. Nobody knew better than he that of all the requirements for producing a painting manual labour was the least. His main preoccupations were creative and scientific. Painting, that is to say the art of observing, was an all-embracing science, and might be identified with seeing, and with the source and foundation of all inquiry into the laws of nature (pp. 30, 32, Trat. 9, 12). She was, therefore, entitled to a dominant position among the Liberal Arts, to whom she was intimately related.

There Geometry had found a seat. There was Music, who with her measure and harmony was believed to be among the forces that governed the universe. There was Astronomy, the science of the harmonious arrangement of the stars in their spheres, who in turn was closely allied to optics and perspective (p. 31, Trat. 17,). It was evident that Painting belonged here.

These mathematical arts were more akin to science than those founded on ethics and logic (p. 57, Trat. 19). With these, too, Painting could compete. If Poetry as an ally of Rhetoric had gained admittance to the Liberal Arts by accepting the role of teacher and moralist, Painting had as good a claim, for she had bowed in the same service: she, too, could delight and elevate.

All the texts in the *Paragone* share in the one theme—'the superiority of painting over all other arts'.

Leonardo refrained from vindicating Sculpture. On the contrary, he looked upon her as a rival. For although she had suffered even more from lack of recognition than Painting in ancient times, she was now contributing considerably towards the revival of classical art, and was represented by great artists, who could speak on her behalf.

The plea for the admission of Painting to the Liberal Arts became a favourite topic with artists and literary men. The wrong which she had suffered by her subordinate position even disturbed a poet's dreams. Francesco Lancilotti in his poem entitled *Trattato di Pittura* (Rome, 1509) described how Painting appeared to him in a vision as a powerful woman descending from heaven saying: 'You must know that what displeases me most is that I am not placed among the seven Liberal Arts.'

At this time Raphael was painting his fresco of the School of Athens where the representatives of the seven Liberal Arts are assembled round Plato and Aristotle in a spacious hall. Entering on the extreme right to join them are two men bearing the features of Raphael and of Sodoma,

who had decorated the ceiling in the stanza and whose art has such affinity with Leonardo's. Thus Raphael's brush recorded the entrance of Painting into the august assembly.

The following quotation from the *Trattato de Pintura Antiqua* (1558) by the Portuguese painter Francisco da Hollanda will show that Leonardo's conception had taken root. In a conversation in the presence of the learned Vittoria Colonna, Michelangelo is represented as saying:

'I sometimes think and imagine that I can find among men but one art or science, that of drawing or painting from which all others spring. For if one considers well all that is done in this life one will find that every man unconsciously is engaged in painting this world both in creating and producing new forms and figures, in dressing variously, in building, and filling spaces with buildings and houses, in cultivating the fields and ploughing the land. I do not mention the arts and professions, of which painting is the fountain head . . . they all flow from the great flood which in ancient days overwhelmed all things in its might as is seen in the works of the Romans which all spring from the art of painting. . . . When they were masters of the world, the art of painting was universal ruler and mistress of all works and arts and sciences.'

No professed protagonist of Painting could have made a more sweeping statement in her favour than this panegyric put into the mouth of Michelangelo by one of his admirers. It reflects the victory which had been gained for the cause. Painting was no longer pleading for admittance to the Liberal Arts: she was the mistress of them all.

The great Italian artists had ceased to be regarded as mere craftsmen, and were being honoured by popes, emperors, and princes. Vasari in a letter to Vincenzo Borghini, dated 1566, was glad of it: 'I have lived to see Art rise suddenly and free herself of knavery and beastliness.'

Soon afterwards the medieval guilds were replaced by academies and the separation of the Fine Arts from the crafts took effect for better and for worse. In 1577 the old Guild of St. Luke in Rome was supplanted by the Academy of the same name with Federigo Zuccaro, the philosophizing painter, as its first director. Other centres in Italy followed suit.

Meanwhile France was awakening to the importance of the arts. In 1648 the Académie Royale de Peinture et Sculpture was opened in Paris. It aimed at setting down the principles of the Fine Arts for the systematic training of students; and according to the report of the secretary, Henri Testelin, Leonardo's treatise on Painting, which was published in Paris in 1651, was the first book consulted. But although

the Fine Arts were recognized as worthy of study by learned men, the ancient prejudice against manual labour persisted among French academicians, as the following quotation from the work of one of their original members shows.

In the preface to his *Entretiens sur les vies et les ouvrages des plus excellents peintres anciens et modernes* (Paris, 1666) André Félibien writes:

'Il faudrait diviser ce long et laborieux ouvrage en trois parties principales. La première qui traiterait de la composition comprendrait presque toute la théorie de l'art. Les deux autres parties qui parleraient du dessin et du coloris ne regardent que la pratique et appartiennent à l'ouvrier, ce qui les rend moins nobles que la première qui est toute libre et que l'on peut savoir sans être peintre.'[1]

Theory came first, and artists were expected to conform. The academies became centres of intellectual precepts, remote from Leonardo's ideas which had inspired the movement at the start.[2]

These same ideas were meanwhile also revolutionizing science; and here the ancient and scholastic conceptions could not for long resist the new current. The birth of modern science was at hand. By identifying Painting with science and by attacking the Liberal Arts for their exclusiveness, Leonardo had supported a movement which was eventually to lead to the dethronement of the humanities and the installation of science in their stead in modern education. But it was science which won the victory. His beloved art of Painting did not profit by this success.

[1] According to Leonardo the creation of a work of art was far superior to scientific theories, see p. 21.

[2] Compare R. vol. i, p. 10 f., and Henry Jouin, *Conférences de l'Académie royale de peinture et de sculpture*, Paris 1883. Antoine Coypel in his discourse delivered in 1720 says: 'with how much diverse knowledge must not the painter's mind be fitted out? Not only should he have a generous acquaintance with the humanities, he should also be somewhat of a rhetorician, that he may use the same rules as the orator so that, like him, he may be able to teach, to please, and to touch the heart.... Not only must he be filled with the same spirit that animates poetry, but he must of necessity know its rules, which are the same as those of painting....'

I

PAINTING AND SCIENCE

a. THE SCIENCE OF PAINTING

'Quoi de plus loin de nous que l'ambition déconcertante d'un Léonard, qui considérant la Peinture comme un suprême but ou une suprême démonstration de la connaissance, pensait qu'elle exigeât l'acquisition de l'omniscience et ne reculait pas devant une analyse générale dont la profondeur et la précision nous confondent?'—PAUL VALÉRY.
'Painting is a science and should be pursued as an inquiry into the laws of nature.'—JOHN CONSTABLE.

ONE of Leonardo's arguments in support of Painting was that it was based on science. He not only applied the methods of scientific research to its subject-matter,[1] he also considered that technique and execution should be based on science.

Considering that at his time no clear distinctions were drawn between art, science, and philosophy, it is surprising to find how near his conception of what true science should be came to modern standards. He put forward as the first prerequisite of true science that it should be based on experience.[2] He was sure that in art as in science there is only one honest method—the experimental. All *a priori* affirmations are dubious. One must descend to technical considerations. Then only can one judge.

Experience then was the starting-point and in the case of painting it was acquired through the sense of sight. Leonardo followed the theory originally propounded by Aristotle, and which was accepted in his

---

[1] Compare p. 6.

[2] In insisting on the importance of testing knowledge by experience and by the senses Leonardo was the forerunner of Francis Bacon and Thomas Campanella, who a century later exposed the shortcomings of the scholastic system and recommended experimental methods. He may have been reinforced in his opinions by Roger Bacon's *Opus Majus*, a work which he seems to have known (see R. 1484), for there he might have found an early confirmation of his point of view that without experience nothing can be known with certainty and that mere arguments are no proof:

'Without experience nothing can be suffi-

ciently known. For there are two modes of acquiring knowledge, namely, by reasoning and experience. Reasoning draws a conclusion and makes us grant the conclusion, but does not make the conclusion certain, nor does it remove doubt so that the mind may rest on the intuition of truth, unless the mind discovers it by the path of experience' (*Opus Majus*, vi. 1). Thus wrote Roger Bacon as early as 1266 in opposition to the trend of thought of his day, when logic was considered the principal door to knowledge and training in logical arguments was the most essential course at the universities. But there was, after all, no need for Leonardo to refer to Roger Bacon's writings.

time, that the five senses transmitted their impressions to the *sensus
communis* as to a centre where they were judged. He sometimes refers
to it as *occhio tenebroso*, the eye closed to external light (p. 50, Trat. 15).
The five senses were ranged in the order of nobility. First came vision,
the supreme sense on which painting depends and which had engendered
science. It perceived ten different qualities—darkness, light, colour,
body, shape, place, distance, nearness, movement, and rest (p. 58, Trat.
20). The order is suggestive of a process of evolution: at the beginning
light invades darkness revealing colour and the surface of bodies, which
are placed at certain distances, nearer and farther away, and which are
expressive of movement and rest. Their representation necessitated the
study of *clair-obscur* and illumination, of aerial and linear perspective,
anatomy and the mechanics of movement.[1]

b. GEOMETRY AND PAINTING

'Painting extends over works human as well as divine in so far as they are bound by surfaces.'—
LEONARDO.

Let us now proceed to another prerequisite of true science. No human
investigation can be called truly scientific if it does not pass through
mathematical demonstrations (p. 22, Trat. 1; R. 1158).[2] Greek Geometry
served as a model. The whole edifice of Euclid's *Elements* was erected
in logical sequence on such simple axioms as 'the point that has no
part', 'the line that has length and no breadth', 'the plane that has length
and breadth only'. The science of painting should proceed no less
accurately and logically; and since like geometry it dealt with spatial
relations, it shared with geometry the same axioms. Both began with
the point, the line, the surface. These had no real existence (pp. 23, 24,
Trat. 1, 3, 4). 'The boundaries of bodies are the boundaries of their
planes; and the boundaries of the planes are lines, which do not form
any part of the size of the planes, nor of the atmosphere which sur-
rounds these planes; therefore that which is not part of anything is
invisible, as is proved by geometry' (Trat. 443).

Painting had to do with the surfaces of things, with planes (pp. 30, 67,
Trat. 9, 26). The painter had to express whatever he wished to represent
in terms of planes. They were the constituent elements in all his works,
his building-stones, so to speak. His task resolved itself into a geometric
problem: How to relate the manifold planes which constitute the sur-

---

[1] Compare p. 6.   [2] Compare L. B. Alberti, *Della Pittura* (145).

PLATE V

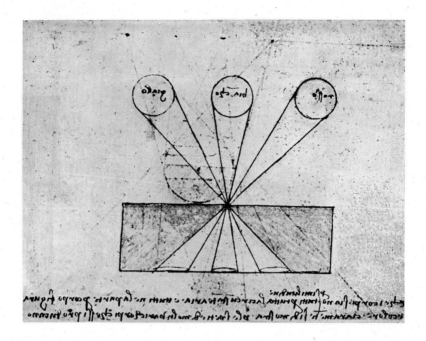

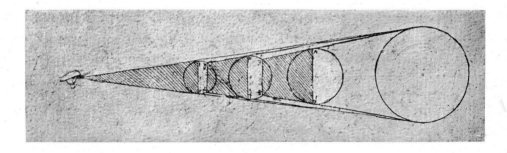

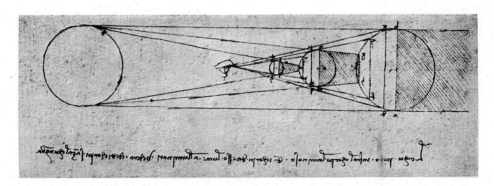

Three diagrams illustrating the theory of Linear Perspective and Light and Shade

faces of objects in space to the one picture plane. This was done by means of perspective, the science of vision which related everything to one point of view. Thus multitude was reduced to unity.

c. SCIENCE AND IMAGINATION

'United with reason, imagination is the mother of the arts and the source of their wonders.'
—FRANCISCO GOYA.

The mathematical conceptions and the study of nature were disciplines that helped the artist in the attainment of an ulterior motive. He was enabled thereby to shape his own images—to create like a god while imitating. 'Truly painting is . . . a true-born child of nature; therefore we may speak of it as related to God' (pp. 32, 57, 74, Trat. 12, 19, 29).[1]

Art is not merely imitation of nature by direct experience (p. 103, Trat. 39); it is an act of creation, which is far superior to the science which precedes it (p. 27, Trat. 33). What Leonardo expressed by his art could not be fathomed by geometry, which dealt with quantities, and not with the beauty of the world (p. 31, Trat. 17). A science can be handed down from master to pupil; but painting cannot be taught to those not favoured by nature (p. 28, Trat. 8).

There is in these thoughts, spontaneously expressed by a sensitive artist about his own work, an imaginative strain which may be compared and related to the Platonic theories of somewhat later writers who describe the ideal beauty conceived by the artist as having its source in God.[2] The 'Idea' in the artist's mind is there compared to the pattern in the mind of God when He created the world.

Although Leonardo did not use the term 'Idea', a similar conception is sometimes implied. He called the science of Painting a deity (p. 63, Trat. 23). The painter according to him was free to use his imagination and to create whatever he wished. 'He can be Lord and God thereof' (p. 51, Trat. 13).[3]

[1] Dante had said that, because art followed nature as the student follows his master, it may be called the grandchild of God, 'si che vostr' arte a Dio quasi è nipote' (*Inferno*, xi. 105-8). Until the eighteenth century the Academy of Design in Florence had as motto, 'A Dio quasi nipote.'

[2] Lomazzo, *Idea del Tempio della Pittura*, 1590; Federico Zuccaro, *L'Idea de' pittori, scultori ed architetti*, 1607; Bellori, *L'Idea del pittore, dello scultore a dell' architetto*, a lecture given to the Accademia di San Luca and printed as introduction to his *Vite de' pittori, scultori et architetti*, 1672; compare Erwin Panofsky, *Idea*, 1924.

[3] Compare Coleridge's definition of imagination: 'The primary "IMAGINATION" I hold to be the living Power and prime Agent of all human perception, and as a repetition in the finite mind of the eternal act of creation in the infinite "I AM"' (*Biographia Literaria*, xiii).

He shared this freedom to invent with the poet.[1] And this leads to the consideration of the content of pictures, where Painting and Poetry had to deal with kindred problems. For just as Painting created beings expressive of life and action in space, so Poetry created beings in words (p. 55, Trat. 19). Emerson's description of a poem may also be said to apply to a painting by Leonardo: 'It is not metres, but a metre-making argument, that makes a poem—a thought so passionate and alive, like a spirit of a plant or an animal, it has an architecture of its own, and adorns nature with a new thing.'

In the following chapter we shall quote Leonardo's views regarding the similarities and differences of the two arts in their methods of appeal, their aims, their means of expression, and their spheres of action; and we shall compare and relate these views to the current classical tradition and to later developments.

PARTE PRIMA

LIBRO DI PITTURA DI M. LIONARDO DA VINCI
Pittore et Scultore Fiorentino

Trat. 1][2]

SE LA PITTURA È SCIENTIA O NÒ

Scientia è detto quel discorso mentale, il quale ha origine da suoi ultimi princípij, de' quali in natura null' altra cosa si può trovare, che sia parte d'essa scientia, come nella quantità continua, cioè la scientia di Geometria, la quale comminciando dalla superfitie de' corpi, si trova

FIRST PART

BOOK ON PAINTING OF LEONARDO DA VINCI
Florentine Painter and Sculptor

I

IS PAINTING A SCIENCE OR NOT?

Science is an investigation by the mind which begins with the ultimate origin of a subject beyond which nothing in nature can be found to form part of that subject. Take, for example, the continuous quantity[3] in the science of geometry: if we begin with the surface of a body we find that it is derived from

---

[1] Compare p. 55, Trat. 19, footnote 2, and p. 51, Trat. 15. Writing in Leonardo's time, the Platonist Girolamo Fracastoro of Verona (1478–1553) compared the painter's creation to the poet's invention: 'The poet considers a thing solely in its universal relations. . . . The poet is like the painter who does not seek to imitate this and that particular feature, and not as they happen to be with all their defects in them; but, having contemplated the universal and most beautiful idea framed by the creator, the poet creates things as they ought to be.' Naugerius, *Sive De*

Poetica Dialogus, 1555, p. 339.

[2] The number of the chapter in Ludwig's standard edition of the Codex Urbinas 1270 appears in the left margin after the Letters 'Trat.'.

[3] Leonardo's repeated references to 'continuous' and 'discontinuous' quantities refer to a classification first made by Aristotle (Categ. 6) which distinguished between arithmetic and geometry as dealing with discontinuous and continuous quantities respectively, that is to say, with numbers and with magnitudes.

havere origine nella linea, termine di essa superfitie; et in questo non restiamo sodisfatti, per che noi conosciamo la linea havere termine nel punto, et il punto esser quello, del quale null' altra cosa può essere minore. Dunque il punto è il primo principio della Geometria, et niuna altra cosa può essere ne in natura, ne in mente humana, che possa dare principio al punto, perche, se tu dirai, nel contatto fatto sopra una superfitie da una ultima acuità della punta delo stile, quello essere creatione del punto, questo non è vero; ma diremo, questo tale contatto essere una superfitie, che circonda il suo mezzo, et in esso mezzo è la residentia del punto. E tal' punto non è della matteria d'essa superfitie, ne lui, ne tutti li punti de'l universo sono in potentia, ancor che sieno uniti, dato che si potessero unire, comporrebbono parte alcuna d'una superfitie. E dato, che tu te immaginassi, un tutto essere composto di mille punti, qui dividendo alcuna parte da essa quantità di mille, si può dire molto bene, che tal parte sia equale al suo tutto; e questo si prova col zero, ovver' nulla, cioè la decima figura de la aritmeticha, per la quale si figura un' O per esso nullo, il quale posto dopo la unità il fa dire dieci, e se porrai due dopo tale unità, dirà cento, e così infinitamente crescerà sempre dieci volte il numero, dove esso s'aggionge; e lui in se non vale altro, che nulla, e tutti li nulli dell' universo sono equali a un sol nulla inquanto alla loro sustantia e valetudine.

Nissuna humana investigatione si puo dimandare vera scientia, se essa non passa per le matematiche dimostrationi e se tu dirai, che le scientie, che principiano e finischono nella mente habbiano verità, questo non si concede, ma si niega, per molte raggioni e prima, che in tali discorsi mentali non accade esperientia, sanza la quale nulla da di se certezza.

lines, the boundaries of this surface. But we do not let the matter rest there, for we know that the line (in its turn) is terminated by points, and that the point is that (ultimate unit) than which there can be nothing smaller. Therefore the point is the first beginning of geometry, and neither in nature nor in the human mind can there be anything which can originate the point.

For if you say that a point is formed by the contact of the finest conceivable pen with a surface, this is not true. But we may assume such contact to be a surface round a centre and in this centre the point may be said to reside. And the point does not partake of the substance of the surface. Neither this nor all potential points of the universe united, if such a union were possible, could form part of any surface. And supposing you imagined a whole composed of a thousand points and divided some part of this quantity by a thousand, it could very well be said that this thousandth part would be equal to its whole. And the point may be compared to zero or nought, the tenth cipher in arithmetic, which is denoted by an O. If placed after the unit we call it ten; if two are placed after the unit we call it hundred; and so on to infinity, the number being always increased ten times by adding a nought. Yet the nought itself is worth no more than nothing; and all the noughts of the universe are equal to one single nought both as regards their substance and their value.

No human investigation can be called true science without passing through mathematical tests, and if you say that the sciences which begin and end in the mind contain truth, this cannot be conceded, and must be denied for many reasons. First and foremost because in such mental discourses experience does not come in, without which nothing reveals itself with certainty.

Trat. 3] 2

DEL PRIMO PRINCIPIO DELLA SCIENTIA DELLA PITTURA

THE FIRST BEGINNING OF THE SCIENCE OF PAINTING

Il principio della scientia della pittura è il punto; il secondo è la linea; il terzo è la superfitie; il quarto è il corpo, che si veste di tal superfitie. e questo è in quanto à quello, che si fingie, cioè esso corpo, che si fingie, perche in vero la pittura nò s'estende più oltra, che la superfitie, per la quale si fingie il corpo, figura di qualonque cosa evidente.

The science of painting begins with the point, then comes the line, the plane comes third, and the fourth the body in its vesture of planes. This is as far as the representation of objects goes.[1] For painting does not, as a matter of fact, extend beyond the surface and it is by these surfaces that it represents the shapes of all visible things.

Trat. 4] 3

PRINCIPIO DELLA SCIENTIA DELLA PITTURA

THE FIRST PRINCIPLE OF THE SCIENCE OF PAINTING

La superfitie piana ha tutto il suo simulacro in tutta l'altra superfitie piana, che li sta per obietto. Provasi, e sia rs la prima superfitie piana, e oq sia la seconda superfitie piana posta a riscontro alla prima. Dico ch'essa prima superfitie rs è tutta in oq superfitie, e tutta in o, e tutta in q, e tutta in p; perchè rs è bassa dell'angolo, o, e dell'angolo p, e cosi d'infiniti angoli fatti in oq.

The plane surface has its complete counterpart in the whole of the other plane surface which faces it.[2] Proof: Let rs be the first plane surface, and oq the second plane surface facing the first. I say that the whole of the first plane surface rs is in the plane oq, and also in o and in q, and in p, because rs is the base of the angle at o and of the angle at p and of the infinite number of angles made on oq.

Trat. 5] 4

DEL SECONDO PRINCIPIO DELLA PITTURA

OF THE SECOND PRINCIPLE OF PAINTING

Il secondo principio della pittura è l'ombra del corpo, che per lei si fingie. e di questa ombra daremo li suoi principii, e con quelli procederemo nell'isculpir la predetta superfitie.

The second principle of painting concerns the shading of bodies by means of which objects are represented (plastically). We shall give the principles of shading which are to be followed when modelling the aforesaid surface.

[1] 'The plane, the volume, the value, which determine shape and colour constitute the only true "subject" of Cézanne's painting'. (Élie Faure.)

[2] The two planes here referred to are the plane formed by the reflection of nature as seen by the eye and the surface of the painting.

Trat. 6] **5**

<table>
<tr><td>

IN CHE S'ESTENDE LA SCIENTIA DELLA
PITTURA

La scientia della pittura s'estende in
tutti li colori delle superfitie e figure de'
corpi da quelle vestiti et à le loro pro-
pinquità e remotioni con li debiti gradi
di diminuitioni, secondo li gradi delle
distantie. e questa scientia è madre della
prospettiva, cioè linee visuali, la qual
prospettiva si divide in tre parti. e di
queste la prima contiene solamente li
lineamenti de corpi; la seconda della
diminutione de colori nelle diverse dis-
tantie, la terza della perdita della congion-
tione de corpi in varie distantie, ma la
prima, che sol' s'estende nelli lineamenti
e termini de corpi, è detto dissegno,
cioè figuratione di qualonque corpo. da
questa n'esce un altra scientia, che
s'estende in ombra e lume, o' vuoi dire
chiaro e scuro, la qual scientia è di gran
discorso. ma quella delle linee visuali
ha partorito la scientia dell' astronomia,
la quale è semplice prospettiva, perche
son tutte linee uisuali e piramidi tag-
liate.

</td><td>

WHERETO THE SCIENCE OF PAINTING
EXTENDS

The science of painting deals with all
the colours of the surfaces of bodies and
with the shapes of the bodies thus en-
closed; with their relative nearness and
distance; with the degrees of diminu-
tions required as distances gradually in-
crease; moreover, this science is the
mother of perspective, that is, of the
science of visual rays.[1]

Perspective is divided into three parts,
of which the first deals only with the
line-drawing of bodies; the second with
the toning down of colours as they
recede into the distance; the third with
the loss of distinctness of bodies at
various distances.

Now the first part which deals only
with lines and contours of bodies is
called drawing, that is to say, the figura-
tion of any body. From it springs
another science that deals with shade
and light, also called chiaroscuro, which
requires much explanation. But the
science of the visual rays has given birth
to the science of astronomy, which is
simply a form of perspective since it
entirely depends on visual rays and sec-
tions of pyramids.

</td></tr>
</table>

Trat. 33] **6**

<table>
<tr><td>

QUALE SCIENTIA È MECCANICA, E QUALE
NON È MECCANICHA

Dicono quella cognitione esser mec-
canicha, la quale è partorita dall' esperi-
entia, e quella essere scientifica, che
nasce e finisce nella mente, e quella

</td><td>

WHICH SCIENCE IS MECHANICAL AND
WHICH IS NOT?

They say that knowledge born of ex-
perience is mechanical, but that know-
ledge born and consummated in the
mind is scientific, while knowledge

</td></tr>
</table>

<table>
<tr><td>

[1] The pyramid of sight is also an important
feature of Leon Battista Alberti's *Treatise on
Painting*. The theory had its origin in Plato's
description of the eye (*Timaeus*, 45). Alberti's
original Latin text was not published until
1546, but even if Leonardo had not actually
seen Alberti's book (it is not mentioned in his

</td><td>

manuscripts; see Solmi, *Le Fonti*, p. 37), he
must have heard of its contents. His friend
Luca Pacioli was in his youth Alberti's guest
in Rome for several months and may have
been a connecting link between the two great
protagonists of the Renaissance. Compare Sir
Kenneth Clark, *L. B. Alberti on Painting*, p. 16.

</td></tr>
</table>

E

essere semimeccanicha, che nasce dalla scientia e finisce nella operatione manuale. ma à me pare, che quelle scientie sieno vane e piene di errori, le quali non sonno nate dall' esperientia, madre di ogni certezza, e che non terminano in nota esperientia, cioè, che la loro origine, ò mezzo, ò fine non passa per nessun de' cinque sensi. (e se noi dubitiamo della certezza di ciascuna cosa, che passa per li sensi, quanto maggiormente dobbiamo noi dubitare delle cose ribelle ad essi sensi, come della asentia di Dio e dell' anima e simili, per le quali sempre si disputa e contende, e veramente accade, che sempre dove mancha la raggione, suplisse le grida, la qual cosa non accade nelle cose certe.

Diremo per questo che dove si grida non è vera scientia, perchè la verità ha un sol termine, il quale essendo publicato il lettiggio resta in eterno distrutto, e s'esso litiggio resurge, ella è bugara e confusa scientia, e non certezza rinata.) ma le vere scientie son quelle, che la sperientia ha fatto penetrare per li sensi e posto silentio alla lingua de' litiganti, e che non pasce di sogno li suoi inuestigatori, ma sempre sopra li primi veri e noti principij procede successivamente e con vere seguentie insino al fine, come si dinota nelle prime matematiche, cioè numero e misura, detta aritmeticha e geometria, che trattano con soma verità della quantità discontinua e continua. Qui non si arguirà, che due tre faccino più o men che sei, nè che un triangolo abbia li suoi angoli minori di duoi angoli retti, ma con etterno silentio resta distrutta ogni arguitione, e con pace sono fruite dalli loro divoti, il che far non possono le buggiarde scientie mentali. e se tu dirai tali scientie vere e note

¹ Compare R. 12, 21, 1210.

born of science and culminating in manual work is semi-mechanical. But to me it seems that all sciences are vain and full of errors that are not born of experience, mother of all certainty, and that are not tested by experience, that is to say, that do not at their origin, middle, or end pass through any of the five senses. (For if we are doubtful about the certainty of things that pass through the senses how much more should we question the many things against which these senses rebel, such as the nature of God and the soul and the like, about which there are endless disputes and controversies. And truly it so happens that where reason is not, its place is taken by clamour. This never occurs when things are certain. Therefore, where there are quarrels, there true science is not; because truth can only end one way—wherever it is known, controversy is silenced for all time, and should controversy nevertheless again arise, then our conclusions must have been uncertain and confused and not truth which is reborn.)¹ All true sciences are the result of experience which has passed through our senses, thus silencing the tongues of litigants. Experience does not feed investigators on dreams, but always proceeds from accurately determined first principles, step by step in true sequences, to the end;² as can be seen in the elements of mathematics founded on numbers and measures called arithmetic and geometry, which deal with discontinuous and continuous quantities with absolute truth. Here no one argues as to whether twice three is more or less than six or whether the angles of a triangle are less than two right angles. Here all argument is destroyed by eternal silence and these sciences can be enjoyed by their devotees in peace. This the deceptive purely speculative sciences cannot achieve. If

² Compare Aristotle, Nic. Ethics, vi. 3–6.

essere di spetie di meccaniche, imperochè non si possono finire se nò manualmente, io dirò il medesimo di tutte l'arti, che passano per le mani delli scrittori, le quale è di spetie di dissegno, membro della pittura; e l'astrologia e l'altre passano per le manuali operationi; ma prima sono mentali, com' è la pittura, la quale è prima nella mente del suo speculatore e non po pervenire alla sua perfettione senza la manuale operatione. della qual pittura li suoi scientifici e veri principij, prima ponendo che cosa è corpo ombroso, e che cosa è ombra primitiva et ombra deriuatiua, e che cosa è lume, cioè tenebre, luce, colore, corpo, figura, sito, remotione, propinquità, moto e quieta, le quali solo con la mente si comprendono senza opera manuale. e questa fia la scientia della pittura, che resta nella mente de' suoi contemplanti. della quale nasce poi l'operatione assai più degna della predetta contemplatione o scientia.

you say that these true sciences that are founded on observation must be classed as mechanical because they do not accomplish their end, without manual work, I reply that all arts that pass through the hands of scribes are in the same position, for they are a kind of drawing which is a branch of painting.

Astronomy and the other sciences also entail manual operations although they have their beginning in the mind, like painting, which arises in the mind of the contemplator but cannot be accomplished without manual operation. The scientific and true principles of painting first determine what is a shaded object, what is direct shadow, what is cast shadow, and what is light, that is to say, darkness, light, colour, body, figure, position, distance, nearness, motion, and rest. These are understood by the mind alone and entail no manual operation; and they constitute the science of painting which remains in the mind of its contemplators; and from it is then born the actual creation, which is far superior in dignity to the contemplation or science which precedes it.

7

QUALE SCIENTIA È PIU UTILE, ET IN CHE CONSISTE LA SUA UTILITÀ

Quella scientia è più utile, della quale il suo frutto è più communicabile, e cosi per contrario è meno utile ch'è meno communicabile. La pittura ha il suo fine communicabile a tutte le generationi de l'universo, perchè il suo fine è subietto della virtù visiva; e non passa per l'orecchio al senso comune col medesimo modo, che vi passa per il vedere, donque questa non ha bisogno de interpreti di diverse lingue, come hanno le lettere, e subito ha satisfatto alla humana spetie, non altrimenti, che si facciano le cose prodotte dalla natura. e non che alla spetie humana, ma alli altri animali, come s'è manifestato in una pittura imitata da

WHICH SCIENCE IS THE MORE USEFUL AND IN WHAT DOES ITS USEFULNESS CONSIST?

That science is the most useful whose fruit is most communicable, and conversely, that is less useful which is less communicable. The result of painting is communicable to all generations of the universe, because it depends on the visual faculty; the way through the ear to our understanding is not the same as the way through the eye; because the latter way has no need of interpreters for the various languages as letters have, and thus painting gives satisfaction at once to mankind, in the same way as things created by nature, and not only to mankind but also to animals, as was shown by a painting

uno padre di famiglia, alla quale faceva carezze li piccioli figliuoli, che anchora erano nelle fascie, e similmente il cane e gatta della medesima casa, ch'era cosa maravigliosa a considerare tale (MS. si fatto) spectacolo.

La pittura rapresenta al senso con più verità e certezza l'opere di natura, che non fanno le parolle, o' le lettere, ma le lettere rappresentano con più verità le parole al senso che non fa la pittura. ma diremo essere più mirabile quella scientia, che rapresenta l'opere di natura, che quella, che rapresenta l'opere del' operatore, cioè, l'opere degli homini, che sono le parole, com' è la poesia e simili, che passano per la humana lingua.

representing the father of a family which was caressed by infants who were still in their swaddling clothes, and also by the dog and the cat in the same house—a spectacle marvellous to behold.

Painting presents the works of nature to our understanding with more truth and accuracy than do words or letters; but letters represent words with more truth than does painting. But we affirm that a science representing the works of nature is more wonderful than one representing the works of a worker, that is to say, the works of man, such as words in poetry and the like, which are expressed by the human tongue.

Trat. 9(4)]   7a

Tutte le scientie, che finiscono con parole, hanno si presto morte, come vita, eccetto la sua parte manuale cioè lo scrivere, ch'è parte mechanica.

All sciences which end in words are dead the moment they come to life, except for their manual part, that is to say, the writing, which is the mechanical part.[1]

Trat. 8]   8

DELLE SCIENTIE IMITABILI

OF IMITABLE SCIENCES

Le scientie, che sonno imitabili, sono in tal modo, che con quelle il discepolo si fa equale all' autore, e similmente fa il suo frutto. queste sonno utili allo imitatore, ma non sonno di tanta eccellenzia, quanto sono quelle, che non si possonno lasciare per heredità, come l'altre sustantie. infra le quali la pittura è la prima. questa non s'insegna à chi natura no 'l concede, come fan le matematiche, delle quali tanto ne piglia il discepolo, quanto il maestro gli ne legge. questa non si copia, come si fa le lettere, che tanto vale la copia, quanto l'origgine. questa non s'impronta, come si fa la scultura, della quale tal' è la impressa qual' è la origgine, in quanto alla virtu de l'opera; questa non fa infiniti figlioli, come fa li libri

In imitable sciences the student can attain equality with the master and can produce similar fruit. These sciences are useful to the imitator, but they are not of such excellence as those which cannot be passed on in heritage like other goods. Among inimitable sciences painting comes first. It cannot be taught to those not endowed by nature like mathematics, where the pupil takes in as much as the master gives. It cannot be copied like letters where the copy has the same value as the original. It cannot be moulded as in sculpture where the cast is equal in merit to the original; it cannot be reproduced indefinitely as is done in the printing of books. It remains peerless in its nobility; alone it does honour to its author, remaining unique and

[1] Compare Plato, *Phaedrus*, 275d.

stampati. questa sola si resta nobile, questa sola honora il suo autore e resta pretiosa et unica, e non partorisce mai figliuoli eguali à se. e tal singularità la fa più eccellente, che quelle, che per tutto sono publicate. hor non uedemo noi li grandissimi Re dell' Oriente andare velati e coperti, credendo diminuire la famma loro col publicare e divulgare le loro presentie? hor non si vede le pitture rappresentatrici delle divine deità esser al continuo tenute coperte con copriture di grandissimi prezzi? e quando si scoprano, prima si fa grande solennità ecclesiatiche di vari canti con diversi suoni e nello scoprire la gran moltitudine de' populi, che quivi concorrono, immediate si gittano a terra, quella adorando e pregando, per cui tale pittura è figurata, del' aquisto della perduta sanità e della etterna salute, non altra mente, che se tale iddea fusse li presente in uita? questo non accade in nissun' altra scientia, od altra humana opera, e se tu dirai, questa non esser virtù del pittore, ma propria virtù della cosa immitata, si rispondera, che in questo caso la mente de li homini po satisfare, standosi nel letto, e non andare ne' lochi faticosi e pericolosi ne' pellegrinaggi, come al continuo far si vede, ma se pure tai pellegrinaggi al continuo sono in essere, chi li moue sanza necessità? certo tu confesserai, essere tale simulacro, il quale far non po tutte le scritture, che figurar potessino in effigie et in virtù tale Iddea. Adonque pare, che essa Iddea ami tal pittura, et ami, chi l'ama e riverisse, e si diletti d'essere adorata più in quella, che in altra figura di lei immitata, e per quella faccia gratie e doni di salute, secondo il credere di quelli, che in tal loco concoreno.

precious; it never engenders offspring equal to it; and this singleness makes it finer than the sciences which are published everywhere. Do we not see great kings of the East go about veiled and covered because they think they might diminish their fame by showing themselves in public and divulging their presence. Do we not see that pictures representing deity are kept constantly concealed under costly draperies and that before they are uncovered great ecclesiastical rites are performed with singing to the strains of instruments; and at the moment of unveiling the great multitude of peoples who have flocked there throw themselves to the ground, worshipping and praying to Him whose image is represented for the recovery of their health and for their eternal salvation as if the Deity were present in person.

The like does not happen with any other science or any other work of man; and if you assert that it is not due to the merit of the painter but to the subject represented we answer that if that were so men might remain peacefully in their beds provided their imagination were satisfied instead of going to wearisome and perilous places as we see them doing constantly on pilgrimages. And what necessity impels these men to go on pilgrimages? You certainly will agree that the image of the Deity is the cause and that no amount of writing could produce the equal of such an image either in form or in power. It would seem, therefore, that the Deity loves such a painting and loves those who adore and revere it and prefers to be worshipped in this rather than in another form of imitation, and bestows grace and deliverance through it according to the belief of those who assemble in such a spot.

Trat. 9(1)]   **9**

COME LA PITTURA ABRACCIA TUTTE LE
SUPERFITIE DE' CORPI ET IN QUELLE
S'ESTENDE

HOW PAINTING EMBRACES ALL THE SUR-
FACES OF BODIES AND EXTENDS
TO THESE

La pittura sol s'estende nelle superfitie
de' corpi, e la sua prospettiva s'estende
nell' acrescimento e decrescimento de'
corpi e de' lor colori. perche la cosa, che
si rimove dall' occhio perde tanto di
grandezza e di colore, quanto l'acquista
di remotione. adonque la pittura è filo
sofia, perche la filosofia tratta de moto
aumentativo e diminutivo, il quale si
trova nella sopradetta propositione; della
quale faremo la conversa, e diremo: la
cosa ueduta dall' occhio acquista tanto
di grandezza e notitia e colore, quanto
ella diminuisse lo spatio interposto infra
essa e l'occhio, che la vede.

Painting extends only to the surface of
bodies; perspective deals with the increase and decrease of bodies and of their
colouring, because an object as it recedes
from the eye loses in size and colour in
proportion to the increase of distance.

Therefore painting is philosophy, because philosophy deals with the increase
and decrease through motion as set forth
in the above proposition; or we may
reverse the statement and say that the
object seen by the eye gains in size, importance, and colour as the space inter-
posed between it and the eye which sees
it diminishes.

Trat. 9(3)]

Si proua la pittura essere filosofia,
perchè essa tratta del moto de' corpi
nella prontitudine delle loro attioni, e la
filosofia anchora lei s'estende nel moto.

Painting can be shown to be philosophy because it deals with the motion
of bodies in the promptitude of their
actions, and philosophy too deals with
motion.

Trat. 10]   **10**

COME LA PITTURA ABBRACCIA LE SUPER-
FITIE, FIGURE E COLORI DE' CORPI
NATURALI, E LA FILOSOFIA SOL S'ESTENDE
NELLE LOR VIRTÙ NATURALI

PAINTING   EMBRACES   THE SURFACES,
SHAPES, AND COLOURS OF NATURAL
BODIES, AND PHILOSOPHY ONLY EXTENDS
TO THEIR NATURAL PROPERTIES

La pittura s'estende nelle superfitie,
colori e figure di qualonque cosa creata
dalla natura, e la filosofia penetra dentro
alli medesimi corpi, considerando in
quelli le lor proprie virtù. ma non
rimane satisfatta con quella verità, che
fa il pittore, che abbraccia in se la prima
verità, di tali corpi, perchè l'occhio meno
se inganna.

Painting extends to the surfaces, colours, and shapes of all things created by
nature; while philosophy penetrates
below the surface in order to arrive at
the inherent properties, but it does not
carry the same conviction, and in this is
unlike the work of the painter who ap-
prehends the foremost truth of these
bodies, as the eye errs less.

Trat. 17]   II

COME LA SCIENTIA DELLA ASTROLOGIA
NASCE DAL' OCCHIO, PERCHE MEDIANTE
QUELLO È GENERATA

Nissuna parte è nell' Astrologia, che
non sia ufficio delle linee uisuali e
della prospettiua, figliola della pittura,—
perche 'l pittore è quello, che per necessità della sua arte ha partorito essa prospettiua,—et non si po fare per se senza
linee, dentro alle quali linee s'inchiudono
tutte le uarie figure de corpi generati dalla
natura, sanza le quali l'arte del geometra
è orba. E se 'l geometra riduce ogni
superfitie circondata da linee alla figura
del quadrato et ogni corpo alla figura del
cubo, e l'Aritmeticha fa il simile con le
sue radici, cube e quadrate, queste due
scientie non s'estendono, se non alla
notitia della quantità continua e discontinua, ma della qualità non si trauaglia,
la quale è bellezza delle opere di natura
et ornamento del mondo.

HOW THE SCIENCE OF ASTRONOMY IS BORN
OF THE EYE, BECAUSE THROUGH IT THIS
SCIENCE WAS BROUGHT INTO EXISTENCE[1]

There is no part of astronomy that does
not make use of visual lines and of perspective[2]—the child of painting—for it
is the painter who created perspective to
meet the requirements of his art—and
she cannot do without lines which bound
all the various shapes of natural objects;
without lines the art of the geometrician
is blind.

And as the geometrician reduces every
area circumscribed by lines to the square
and every body to the cube; and arithmetic does likewise with its cubic and
square roots, these two sciences do not
extend beyond the study of continuous
and discontinuous quantities; but they
do not deal with the quality of things
which constitutes the beauty of the works
of nature and the ornament of the world.

Trat. 34]   I2

PERCHÈ LA PITTURA NON È CONNUMERATA
NELLE SCIENTIE

Perchè gli scrittori non hanno avuto
notitia della scientia della pittura, non
hanno possuto descriverne li gradi e parti
di quella, e lei medesima non si dimostra
col suo fine nelle parole, essa è restata
mediante l'ignorantia indietro alle predette scientie, non mancando per questo
di sua divinità. e veramente non senza
caggione non l'hanno nobilitata, perchè
per se medesima si nobilita, senza l'aiuto
del' altrui lingue, non altrimente, che si
facciano l'eccellenti opere di natura. et
se li pittori non hanno di lei descritto e
ridottola in scientia, non è colpa della

WHY PAINTING IS NOT NUMBERED AMONG
THE SCIENCES

As the scribes have had no knowledge
of the science of painting they could not
assign to it its rightful place or share; and
painting does not display her accomplishment in words; therefore she was
classed below the sciences, through ignorance—but she does not thereby lose
any of her divine quality.

And truly, it was not without reason
that they did not confer honours upon
her, since she proclaims her own glory
without the help of tongues in the same
way as do the excellent works of nature.
And it is not the fault of painting if
painters have not described their art and

[1] See Plato, *Timaeus*, 47, quoted on p. 34,
note 1.
[2] See John Peckham, *Perspectiva*, where the
sizes of the stars and the relative position of

sun and moon are determined by means of
visual rays; and Roger Bacon, *Opus Majus*, v,
where astronomy is treated as a branch of
optics.

pittura, ella non è per questo meno nobile, poscia che pochi pittori fanno professione di lettere, perchè la lor vita non basta ad intendere quella. per questo haremo noi a dire, che le virtù dell' erbe, pietre et piante non sieno in essere, perchè li huomini non le habbino conosciute? certo no. ma diremo esse erbe restarsi in se nobili, senza lo aiuto delle lingue o' lettere humane.

reduced it to a science, she is not the less noble for that, since few painters profess to be writers because life is too short for the understanding of their art.

Do we deny the existence of the properties of herbs, or stones, or trees because men knew them not? Certainly not, we must admit that these herbs retain their noble qualities without the help of human tongues or writings.

Trat. 12]   13

COME CHI SPREZZA LA PITTURA, NON AMA LA FILOSOFIA, NE LA NATURA

Se tu sprezzarai la pittura, la quale è sola imitatrice di tutte l'opere evidenti di natura, per certo tu sprezzarai una sottile inventione, la quale con filosofica e sottile speculatione considera tutte le qualità delle forme: mare, siti, piante, animali, herbe, fiori, le quali sono cinte d'ombra e lume. e veramente questa è scientia e legittima figlia di natura, perche la pittura è partorita da essa natura; ma per dir più corretto, diremo nipota di natura, perche tutte le cose euidenti sonno state partorite dalla natura, delle quali cose è nata la pittura. Adonque rettamente la chiameremo nipota d'essa natura et parente d'Iddio.

HE WHO DEPRECATES PAINTING LOVES NEITHER PHILOSOPHY NOR NATURE[1]

If you despise painting, which is the sole imitator of all visible works of nature, you certainly will be despising a subtle invention which brings philosophy and subtle speculation to bear on the nature of all forms—sea and land, plants and animals, grasses and flowers —which are enveloped in shade and light. Truly painting is a science, the true-born child of nature. For painting is born of nature; to be more correct we should call it the grandchild of nature, since all visible things were brought forth by nature and these, her children, have given birth to painting. Therefore we may justly speak of it as the grandchild of nature and as related to God.[2]

Trat. 9(2)]   13*a*

Chi biasima la pittura, biasima la natura, perche l'opere del pittore rappresentano l'opere d'essa natura, e per questo il detto biasimatore ha carestia di sentimento.

Whoso speaks ill of painting speaks ill of nature, because the works of the painter represent the works of nature, and therefore such a detractor lacks feeling.

[1] Compare the elder Philostratos' Eἰκόνες, 'Whoever does not love Painting, the wise imitator of the Gods, of men and of all nature, whoever does not embrace her does not love truth, and repulses all the wisdom that ever descended on a poet, he even rejects sym-

metry without which neither word nor deed can ever endure.' Pomponius Gauricus applied this saying of Philostratos to sculpture (*De sculptura*, i, p. 104, edition 1886).

[2] Compare p. 21 and Dante, *Inferno*, xi. 105.

COME L'OCCHIO MENO S'INGANNA NELLI
SUOI ESSERCIZII, CHE NISSUN ALTRO SENSO,
ILLUMINOSI O TRASPARENTI ET UNIFORMI
ET MEZZI

HOW THE EYE IS LESS EASILY DECEIVED
THAN ANY OTHER SENSE IN THE EXERCISE
ON OBJECTS REFLECTING LIGHT OR TRANS-
PARENT, (WHICH ARE) ENDS AND MEANS

L'occhio nelle debite distantie e debiti mezzi meno s'inganna nel suo uffitio, che nissun altro senso, perchè vede se non per linee rette, che compongono la piramide, che si fa bassa dell' obbietto, e la conduce à esso occhio, come intendo provare. ma l'orecchio forte s'ingaña nelli siti e distantie delli suoi obbietti, perche non vengono le spetie a lui per rette linee, come quelle dell' occhio, ma per linee tortuose e riflesse, e molte sono le volte, che le remote paiano più vicine, che le propinque mediante li transiti di tali spetie; benche la voce di echo sol' per linee rette si riferiscie à esso senso. l'odorato meno si certifica del sito, donde si causa un' odore; ma il gusto et il tatto, che tocchano l'obbietto, han sola notitia di esso tatto.

Given the proper distances and the required atmospheric conditions, the eye errs less in its function than any other sense, because, as will be shown later, the object is conveyed to the eye along the straight and converging lines of a pyramid, the base of which it forms.

But the ear is apt to be misled in locating and judging the distances of its objects because the lines along which sound travels are not straight like those of the pyramid of sight, but tortuous and bent. And very often distant sounds seem nearer than those close by, owing to the transmission; although the sound of the echo travels to the ear by straight lines only.[1]

The sense of smell is even less able to locate the cause of odours; and the senses of taste and touch must come into actual contact with their objects before they become aware of them.

QUAL È DI MAGGIOR DANNO ALLA SPETIE
HUMANA, O' PERDERE L'OCCHIO, O'
L'ORECCHIO

WHICH IS THE WORSE INJURY TO MANKIND,
THE LOSS OF THE EYE OR THE LOSS OF THE
EAR?

Maggior danno riceuono gli animali per la perdita del uedere, che del udire, per più caggioni; e prima, che mediante di uedere il cibo è ritrouato, donde si debbe nudrire, il quale è necessario a tutti gli animali; el secondo, che per il uedere si comprende il bello delle cose create, massime delle cose, che in ducono all' amore, nel quale il cieco nato non po pigliare per lo audito, perche mai non ebbe nottitia, che cosa fusse bellezza d'alcuna cosa. Restagli l'audito, per il quale solo intende le uoci et parlare

Animals sustain worse injury by losing their sight than their hearing for several reasons; first, they need their sight to secure the nourishment indispensable to all animals; secondly, by sight the beauty of created things is perceived, which are the chief cause of love. He who is born blind cannot replace this experience through the sense of hearing because he has never known what is the beauty of anything. There remains to him the sense of hearing whereby he hears the voices and the speech of men which is composed of the names of all things that

[1] Compare Aristotle, *De audib.* 801; *De Anima*, ii. 8; Cecco d'Ascoli, *L'Acerba*, book iv, ch. 3.

F

humano, nel quale i nomi di tutte le cose, a chi è datto il suo nome. senza la saputa d'essi nomi ben si po uiuere lieto, come si uede nelli sordi nati, cioè li muti, che mediante il disegno, del quale i più de' muti si dilettano. e se tu dirai, che 'l uedere impedisse la fissa e sottile cognitione mentale, conla quale si penetra nelle diuine scientie, et tale impedimento condusse un filosofo à priuarsi del uedere, à questo si risponde, che tal occhio, come signore de sensi, fa suo debito à dare impedimento alli confusi e bugiardi, non scientie, ma discorsi, per li quali sempre con gran gridore e menare de mani si disputa, et il medesimo dourebbe fare l'audito, il quale ne rimane più offeso, perche egli uorrebbe accordo, del quale tutti li sensi s'intricano. E se tal filosofo si trasse gli occhi per leuare l'impedimento alli suoi discorsi, hor pensa, che tal atto fu compagno del ceruello e de' discorsi, perchè tutta fu pazzia. Or non potea egli serarsi gli occhi, quando esso entraua in tale frenesia, e tanto tenerli seṝati, che tal furore si consumasse? Ma pazzo fu l'homo, e pazzo il discorso, e stoltissimo il trarsi gli occhi.

have been given names. But one can live happily without the knowledge of these names as is shown by those born deaf, who, being dumb, make themselves understood by drawing, which most of them enjoy.

And if you say that sight impedes the concentrated and subtle reasoning by which access is gained to the theological sciences; and that because of this impediment a certain philosopher was induced to deprive himself of his sight, the answer is that the eye does its duty as lord of all senses in impeding the confused and mendacious arguments (one cannot call them science), by which they dispute with continued loud clamour and waving of hands. Indeed, the sense of hearing should join the protest, as it is being offended even more than the eye in that longing for harmony in which all senses combine.

And if the philosopher plucked out his eyes in order to remove the impediment to his reasoning you may well think that this deed was a fit companion to his brain and his arguments, because all of it was madness. Might he not have closed his eyes when the frenzy overcame him, and kept them closed until the rage had consumed itself? But the man was mad, and his reasoning was mad, and the plucking out of the eyes was maddest of all.[1]

[1] The need for concentration for elimination of disturbing elements found symbolic expression in the story of the blindness of Democritus and Plato. According to the Christian Platonists transcendental speculation entailed 'the plucking out of the offending eye'. The painter Lomazzo, who himself became blind, says (*Trattato*, vi, c. 65, p. 462), 'Leggesi a questo proposito che Omero, Democrito e Platone da se stessi si privarono della luce degli occhi per meglio e più sottilmente investigare la natura di quello che nella sua mente concetto ed immaginato si avevano.'

Plato's own view on the subject of human vision can be found in the *Timaeus* (47), and it is of interest in comparison with Leonardo's.

'The eyesight is the cause of the greatest benefit to us, inasmuch as none of the accounts now given concerning the Universe would ever have been given if men had not seen the stars or the sun or the heaven. But as it is, the vision of day and night and of months and circling years ... has created the art of number and has given us not only the notion of Time but also means of research into the nature of the Universe. From these we have procured Philosophy in all its range, than which no greater boon ever has come or will come, by divine bestowal into the race of mortals. This

Trat. 15*a*]   15*a*

Qual è colui, che non uoglia prima perdere l'udire, l'odorato e 'l tatto, che 'l uedere? perchè chi perde il uedere, è come un, ch'è scacciato dal mondo, perche egli più no 'l uede, ne nessuna sua cosa. e questa vitta è sorella della morte.

Who would not lose his sense of hearing and the senses of smell and touch as well rather than his sight, because he who loses his sight is like a man chased from the world—for he no longer sees it nor anything of it, and such life is the sister of death.

Trat. 24]   16

DELL' OCCHIO

L'occhio, del quale la bellezza de l'uni-verso è specchiata dalli contemplanti, è di tanta eccellentia, che chi consente alla sua perdita, si priua della rapresentatione di tutte l'opere della natura, per la veduta delle quali l'anima sta contenta nelle humane carceri mediante gli occhi, per li quali essa anima si rapresenta tutte le uarie cose di natura; ma chi li perde, lascia essa anima in una oscura priggione, doue si perde ogni speranza di rivider il sole, luce di tutt' il mondo. e quanti son quelli, d chi le tenebre notturne sono in sommo odio, ma anchora ch'elle sieno di breue uita! o, che farebbono questi, quando tali tenebre fussino compagne della vita loro?

Certo, non è nissuno, che non volesse più tosto perdere l'udito e l'odorato, che l'occhio, la perdita del quale udire consente la perdita di tutte le scientie channo termine nelle parole, e sol fa questo per non perdere la bellezza del mondo, la quale consiste nella superfitie de' corpi, si accidentali, come naturali, li quali si reflettono nel occhio humano.

OF THE EYE

The eye whereby the beauty of the world is reflected by beholders is of such excellence that whoso consents to its loss deprives himself of the representation of all the works of nature. Because we can see these things owing to our eyes the soul is content to stay imprisoned in the human body; for through the eyes all the various things of nature are represented to the soul. Who loses his eyes leaves his soul in a dark prison without hope of ever again seeing the sun, light of all the world; and how many there are to whom the darkness of night is hateful though it is of but short duration; what would they do if such darkness were to be their companion for life?

Certainly there is nobody who would not prefer to lose his hearing and his sense of smell rather than the sight of his eyes. Although in consenting to the loss of hearing he relinquishes all knowledge that depends on words; he only consents to it in order not to lose the beauty of the world, which consists of the surfaces of the bodies with both their accidental and their natural qualities as reflected in the human eye.

I affirm to be the greatest good of eyesight. As for all the lesser goods, why should we celebrate them? He that is no philosopher, when deprived of the sight thereof, may utter vain lamentations' (trans. Archer Hind). The

last sentence was later interpreted to mean that the philosopher should pluck out his eye. Compare *Phaedrus*, 250d, where sight is described as the keenest of all the bodily senses, but wisdom cannot be discerned thereby.

POETRY AND PAINTING[1]

'The fundamental features of reading poetry and appreciating pictures, the features upon which their value depends, are alike. The means by which they are brought about are unlike, but closely analogous critical and technical problems arise for each.'—I. A. RICHARDS.[2]

AN important part of the *Paragone* is devoted to the comparison between Painting and Poetry. From the time when Simonides of Keos (*c.* 500 B.C.) pronounced his saying, quoted by Plutarch, that Painting was mute Poetry and Poetry speaking Painting, to the present day the two arts have often been related to one another. Plato associated them in *Phaedrus* and in *The Republic*. Aristotle, when writing on Poetry, repeatedly compared her to the sister art in order to drive home his argument. Plutarch, Cicero, Quintilian followed suit. The Philostrati began their *Essays on Painting* by calling attention to the affinity of the two arts; and Horace began his *Ars Poetica* by introducing the reader into the painter's studio.

With the revival of interest in classical literature in the Early Renaissance, poets turned to Horace's *Ars Poetica* for guidance. But the humanist writers on Painting had no equivalent *Ars Pictorica* to turn to. They were instead acquainted with the frequent comparisons of Painting with Poetry, and they proceeded to apply recommendations which were intended for one art indiscriminately to another. Pomponius Gauricus, artist and poet, in his treatise on Sculpture (1504) asked: 'Why should we separate these two arts? . . . I feel that they are by their nature related so that they can hardly exist apart from one another.' And he proceeded to trace both back to one common source—to the hieroglyphics of ancient Egypt which combined drawing and writing!

a. EXPRESSION OF EMOTIONS

'That figure is most admirable which by its actions best expresses the spirit that animates it.'—LEONARDO.

According to the classical tradition both poetry and painting were based on imitation. Aristotle attributed the origin of poetry to man's

[1] For a detailed account of the literature on this subject in the post-Renaissance era, Professor Rensselaer W. Lee's 'Ut pictura poesis: The Humanistic Theory of Painting', *Art Bulletin*, xxii (December 1940), published by the College Art Association of America. Karl Borinski, *Die Antike in Poetik und Kunsttheorie*, 1914, contains suggestive references to the subject in classical literature.

[2] *Principles of Literary Criticism*, 1924.

inborn love for imitation, and he considered men in action special subjects for representation (*Poetics* 2, 4, 6). There need be no ulterior motive but that of affording relief to emotions. Horace, on the other hand, advised poets to make use of the imitation of nature in order to lead the hearer's soul where they wished, and they were to do so by emotional appeals, by making men's faces smile on those who smile, and respond to those who weep (*Ars Poetica*, 101). They were to identify themselves with whatever they longed to be or say, and by the expression of their emotions arouse similar feelings in their listeners. The painters achieved their effects by representing figures in telling attitudes like actors on the stage; and Quintilian had to admit that the silent gestures of painting surpassed in efficiency the power of speech (*Inst. Orat.* xi. 3. 65 ff.).

The Early Renaissance followed Horace's advice. The humanist Leon Battista Alberti considered that expression was the all-essential and most difficult task of the painter (*Della Pittura*, pp. 121 ff.). And this is where Leonardo excelled. His works were admired for the expression which he gave to his figures. Their effect on the young Raphael is described by Vasari:

'On becoming acquainted with the works of Leonardo da Vinci, who in the expression he gave to his heads, whether male or female, had no equal, and who surpassed all others in the grace and movement he gave to his figures, Raphael stood confounded in astonishment and admiration, and set himself zealously to the study thereof.'

In his treatise on Painting Leonardo declares that it is one of the painter's most important tasks to adapt the figures to the expression of the required mental attitudes. Physiognomies must reveal the frame of mind; actions must suggest the motives which inspire them. The body was shaped by the spirit; and it is for the painter to reverse the process, so to speak, and to create a body that gives expression to the soul (Trat. 115, 122, 180, 199, 294, 298, 207, 499).

In laying down a plan for his treatise on Anatomy he writes:

'Then in four drawings represent four universal conditions of man—that is Mirth, with various acts of laughter; and describe the cause of laughter; Weeping in various aspects with its causes; Contention, with various acts of killing, flight, fear, ferocity, boldness, murder and everything pertaining to such cases; then represent Labour with pulling, thrusting, carrying, stopping, supporting and such things.' (R. 797.)

As was his custom, Leonardo approached his subject with empirical directness and personal observation. He went about with his sketch-book, observed, and noted down. He studied the gestures of the dumb who had no other means of expression (Trat. 376).

The following descriptions of his methods of study (from contemporary sources) are of interest in this connexion:

Giovanbatista Giraldi (*Discorso intorno al comporre dei romanzi, delle commedie e delle tragedie*, 1554), whose father knew Leonardo, writes:

'When Leonardo wished to paint a figure he first considered what social standing and what nature it was to represent; whether noble or plebeian, gay or severe, troubled or serene, old or young, irritated or tranquil, good or wicked; and when he had made up his mind he went to places where he knew that people of that kind would assemble, and observed their faces, their manners, their dresses, and their movements attentively; and wherever he found what seemed to fit in with what he wanted to do, he noted it down in a little book which he always kept in his belt. After having done this again and again, and feeling satisfied that he had collected sufficient material for the figure which he wished to paint, he would proceed to give it shape and succeeded marvellously.'

G. T. Lomazzo (*Trattato del Arte*, 1585) advises students to follow Leonardo's way of studying the expressions and movements of figures.

'There is a tale told, by men of his time, his servants, that Leonardo once wished to make a picture of some laughing peasant. (Though he did not carry it out but only drew it.) He picked out certain men whom he thought appropriate for his purpose and after getting acquainted with them, arranged a feast for them with some of his friends, and sitting close to them he proceeded to tell the maddest and most ridiculous tales imaginable, making them, who were unaware of his intentions, laugh uproariously. Whereupon he observed all their gestures very attentively and those ridiculous things they were doing, and impressed them on his mind, and, after they had left, he retired to his room and there made a perfect drawing which moved those who looked at it to laughter as if they had been moved by Leonardo's stories at the feast.'

The various studies were then arranged and adapted to form a composition. Each figure was given the pose and expression befitting its part in the motive—be it admiration, reverence, grief, suspicion, fear, joy, or whatever was required (Trat. 285).

PLATE VI

Two men fighting a dragon

PLATE VII

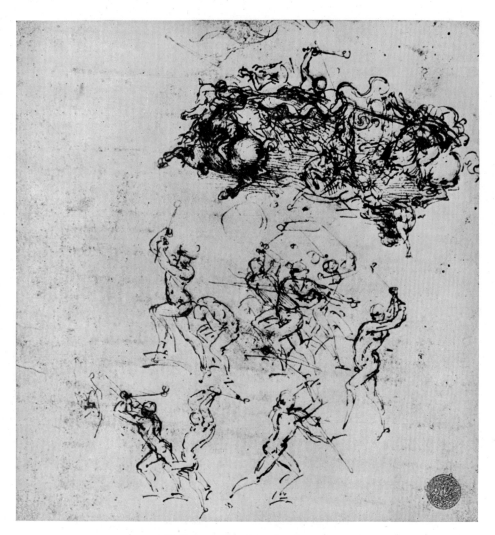

Study for cartoon of Battle of Anghiari

PLATE VIII

Two heads of fighting warriors

To judge by his drawings, Leonardo was able to surprise the most hidden character and the most fleeting sensation. Words fail to describe the smile of La Gioconda. He could also paint a violent action full of fiery passion. In the *Paragone* he challenges the poet to describe a battle, boasting that his tongue would parch with thirst and his body succumb to sleep and hunger before he could achieve what a good painter could present in a single instant to the same audience (Trat. 15 R. 601–2). As we read Leonardo's dire description of a battle with shrieking victors and panic-stricken fugitives, with its clouds of smoke and dust, there rises before us a vision of his Battle of the Standard with its passionate struggle of horses and men.

Leonardo's conception of a composition is impressively revealed in his representation of 'The Last Supper'. A wave of feeling seems to pass through the scene as the effect of Christ's calm announcement of His betrayal by one of His disciples is reflected in their agitated attitudes. The idea of arranging a composition according to its emotional content was taken over and elaborated theoretically by Lomazzo in his description of a Crucifixion where the expression of grief in the mourners at the foot of the Cross must vary in accordance with their relationship to Christ, being intense in the Virgin and in St. John, who were placed in the centre; and gradually subsiding in the figures farther away (Trat. vi. 34). Henceforth problems were no longer approached with Leonardo's empirical directness. Writers on art were busy codifying the knowledge already at hand and formulating theories with which artists were expected to comply; with the result that the intellectual interpretation of a picture tended to overshadow its emotional appeal.

In the seventeenth century the French academician Charles Le Brun proceeded to analyse the passions psycho-physiologically according to Descartes's *Traité des passions de l'âme* (1648). Nicolas Poussin composed his paintings like dramas on a stage. Each figure was given an appropriate dramatic relationship to the central cause of emotion. Each form was made to express its function and purpose. Meanwhile Corneille and Racine embodied the passions of the soul in the characters of their plays according to prescribed rules.

In England ideas were similar. Writing of 'the causes and resorts of that which moves pleasure in a reader', John Dryden said:

'Those springs of human nature are not so easily discovered by every

superficial judge: it requires Philosophy as well as Poetry, to sound the depth of all the passions; what they are in themselves, and how they are to be provoked: and in this science the best poets have excelled. Aristotle raised the fabric of his 'Poetry' from observation of those things in which Euripides, Sophocles and Aeschylus pleased: he considered how they raised the passions, and thence has drawn rules for our imitation.' (*Apology for Heroic Poetry and Poetic Licence.*)

The following lines were addressed by Dryden to Sir Godfrey Kneller, with regrets that he did not devote himself to historical painting but to portraiture:[1]

> Else should we see your noble Pencil trace
> Our unities of Action, Time, and Place;
> A Whole compos'd of Parts, and those the best,
> With ev'ry various character exprest;
> Heroes at large, and at a nearer view,
> Less, and at distance an Ignobler Crew,
> While all the Figures in one Action joyn,
> As tending to Compleat the main Design.

In Painting as in Poetry the classical tradition prevailed. The laws of the three unities to which Dryden refers were ascribed to Aristotle[2] by classicists and were recommended alike to poets and painters. Corneille compared theatrical representation to portraiture and insisted that it must resemble the original. The audience should be made to feel that they were witnessing a real occurrence, which must therefore be represented as coming to pass approximately during the time spent in the theatre in one and the same environment (*Trois discours*, 1660).

It was easier for the painter to conform simultaneously to the three unities of action, time, and place. Leonardo had done so independently and of his own accord. In 'The Last Supper' Christ's prophetic words are uttered in one instant, and the spectator who is viewing the scene from the refectory, which is seemingly an extension of the room where the scene takes place, is drawn into it and made to take part in it. The painter's power to convey his message all at once and independent of time, which Leonardo thought so wonderful, is here made manifest.

[1] Dryden's portrait by Sir G. Kneller is in the National Gallery, London.

[2] Aristotle laid down that the action or plot of a drama be designed to form a unity; but the formal recognition of the unities of time and of place were ascribed to him erroneously, the former being based on the words 'Tragedy tends to fall within a single revolution of the sun or slightly to exceed that limit' (*Poetics* 5); the latter, of which there is no hint in the *Poetics*, dates from Castelvetro's translation published in 1570.

PLATE IX

Drawing of male figures in groups

PLATE X

The Last Supper

b. INSTRUCTION AND DELIGHT

Verily by Beauty is it that we come at Wisdom,
Yet not by Reason at Beauty.   ROBERT BRIDGES

Horace's advice to poets was to influence men towards the good and the fair by displaying it to them. Poetry should at once benefit and delight its readers (*Ars Poetica* 333). It should be a civilizing factor. He called the first poets inspired teachers, as Shelley did in our time: 'Poets according to the circumstances of the age and nation in which they appeared were called in the earlier epochs of the world legislators and prophets; a poet essentially comprises both these characters' (*A Defence of Poetry*). The pedagogical theory of art was flourishing also in the Renaissance. We give below the opinions of outstanding literary men on this subject. Aeneas Sylvius Piccolomini, better known as Pope Pius II, in his treatise *De Liberorum Educatione* (1450), welcomed all that poets can write in praise of virtue and in condemnation of vice, but declared that all other matter in their poems should be left unheeded. Angelo Poliziano, friend of Lorenzo il Magnifico, translator of Homer into Latin, saw in Poetry the source of all civilization (*Nutricia*, 1486). He himself is indebted to her for his entire education. Bernardino Daniello, interpreter of Aristotle and Horace (*Poetica* 1536), admires Poetry because it can teach more pleasantly than any philosopher by concealing useful lessons in fictions and fables as physicians cover pills with sweet coatings. B. Varchi (*Lezioni lette nell' Accademia Florentina*, 1590) says that there are various ways of making men virtuous —by law, by ethics, and by poetry. The last method is the most efficacious because it is the most delightful. 'How difficult it is to withstand the lessons of a beautiful poem where virtuous deeds are rewarded and the wicked punished!'[1]

Owing to the close association of the two arts the subjects of painting were often likened to those of poetry, where ideas play so important a part, and care and attention were given to the intellectual and didactic aspects of pictorial compositions. Leon Battista Alberti in his treatise on Painting (1436) states that pictures are intended to inspire and instruct, and he advised painters to read the poets. They should study from them how to represent their subjects. Had not Phidias learned from Homer how to interpret the divine majesty of Zeus? Raphael

---

[1] Compare Dante, *Paradiso*, xxvii. 91 ff.

G

was considered very adept in representing subjects taken from literature; and in the opinion of experts his paintings surpassed the descriptions which had served him as inspiration.[1]

Leonardo also was ready to vie with poets in the interpretation of their subjects and claimed that Painting was superior in inspiring men to acts of worship and of love. Before a picture of the Deity mankind knelt down in adoration. A painter can create women as lovely as any born of man. He can teach moral lessons most convincingly. Had not Apelles in his famous 'Calumny'[2] shown up an injustice? (pp. 57, 59, Trat. 19, 21). With Dante's *Inferno* in mind, Leonardo declared: 'If Poetry can terrify people by fictions of hell, Painting can do as much by placing the same thing before the eye' (p. 65, Trat. 25). Much of this was doubtless said to have the best of an argument. When, however, he came to consider the subjects of poems he was more critical.

There was a tendency among poets to take the advice to instruct too literally. Among the books in Leonardo's possession was the *Acerba* by Cecco d'Ascoli,[3] a contemporary of Dante and Professor of Astrology at Bologna. As the name of his poem suggests, it deals with things difficult to understand, with astronomy and astrology, with the virtues and vices of men as influenced by the stars, with moral lessons to be learnt from animal life. It was an encyclopaedia in verse. The author boasted that his poem did not narrate vain fictions like Dante's *Divina Commedia*.

Leonardo's contemporary Girolamo Fracastoro of Verona, who was a literary critic and a physician, composed a Latin poem entitled *De*

[1] As an example of Raphael's gift for poetical rendering, Lodovico Dolce (*Dialogo della Pittura*) points to the triumph of Galatea at the Farnesina, and compares it with the poem of Angelo Poliziano:

'Due formosi delfini il carro tirano
Sovr' esso e Galatea che'l fren corregge. . . .'

Shakespeare represented a painter competing with a poet in the first act of *Timon of Athens*:
'A thousand moral paintings I can show
That shall demonstrate these quick blows of
  Fortune
More pregnantly than words.'

The Romantic painters in the nineteenth century were inspired by a similar rivalry. Théo-
phile Gautier said of Delacroix (*Histoire du Romantisme*): 'He penetrates so deeply into the heart of a poem that his rendering is more strongly felt and more significant than the author's original conception', and he quotes Goethe's appreciation of a lithograph by the artist representing Faust and Mephistopheles: 'I must confess that my own idea of this scene was not as perfect' (*Gespräche mit Eckermann*, 29 Nov. 1828).

[2] The subject, taken from Lucian's description of a lost picture by Apelles, occurs frequently in the works of the Renaissance, the most famous example being Botticelli's picture in the Uffizi.

[3] R. 1469.

Morbo Gallico dealing with the symptoms and treatment of the disease. This may have induced him to inquire what distinguishes the poet from other writers in his *Naugerius, sive de poetica dialogus* (1555). 'What is the poet's aim? If it is merely to imitate, there would be no justification for his existence. Nor can his aim be merely to teach and delight as Horace said; for the descriptions of countries, peoples and armies, the accounts of sciences and public events are taken from scientists, and historians, who can teach and delight quite as well as the poets.' Leonardo likewise rebuked the poet for his dependence on other sciences that were not his concern. 'The poet borrows help from sciences altogether distinct from his own art' is his accusation; and he compares him to a pedlar selling other people's wares (p. 79, Trat. 32). He was aware that the painter also went borrowing for the subject-matter of his pictures, and admitted that this aspect showed his art at its weakest (p. 80, Trat. 32). These views coincided in some respects with those of the Aristotelian Lodovico Castelvetro, who about a century later wrote: 'The aim of poetry is to give, by imitation, delight to its listeners, leaving the discovery of the hidden truths of natural philosophy to the philosopher and the scientist.' Painting was to confine itself to the portrayal of external beauty. 'The painter represents the goodness of the body—i.e. beauty; and the poet represents the goodness of the mind—i.e. character.'[1] Such attempts to ascribe separate spheres to the two arts were few and far between. The trend of art criticism in the post-Renaissance was not to differentiate between their educational, moral, and aesthetic aspects. This attitude called for a correct interpretation of their subject-matter, so that their lessons should be founded on truth.

Both Bernardino Daniello (*Poetica* 1536) and Lodovico Dolce (*Dialogo della Pittura*, 1537) recommended extensive studies on the part of poets and painters so that their work should be correct historically and topographically. Landscapes, characters, costumes, manners, must be right. Scientific research, to which Leonardo had attached so much importance, had degenerated into a somewhat pedantic solicitude for truth to fact.

The French Academy inherited these principles regarding representational correctness,[2] though artists were allowed to take liberties in order

---

[1] *Poetica d'Aristotele vulgarizzata et sposta*, 1570; H. B. Charlton, *Castelvetro's Theory of Poetry*, 1913.   [2] Compare p. 17, note 2.

to attain 'a higher truth', since science thus grafted on art seemed to interfere with the accomplishment of its own particular purpose.

Sir Joshua Reynolds, first President of the Royal Academy, felt bound to protest: 'Some writers upon art suppose that such a body of universal and profound knowledge is requisite that the enumeration of its kinds is enough to frighten a beginner' (Discourse VII). In an address delivered to his students in 1786 he recommended the comparison of the arts:

'To enlarge the boundaries of the art of painting, as well as fix its principles, it will be necessary, that *that* art and *those* principles should be considered in their correspondence with the principles of the other arts which, like this, address themselves primarily and principally to the imagination. When those connected and kindred principles are brought together to be compared, another comparison will grow out of this; that is, the comparison of them all with those of human nature, whence arts derive the materials upon which they are to produce their effects' (Discourse XIII).

He condemned the servile imitation of nature by painters, and encouraged them to imitate the poets and use their imagination.

In the nineteenth century the Romantic movement rose against the Academic rules and formulas which were stifling the expression of emotion in literature and art. A loose rein was given to intense and passionate feeling which was considered more important than correctness of form.[1] The reaction that followed led back towards principles of structure. The artist was to concentrate on perfection of form; and content would result therefrom. It was evidently easier to live up to this principle in Painting than in Poetry, where the alinement of words had also to consider their meaning (see p. 49, Trat. 2); and it was still easier in instrumental music which could be non-descriptive. Whistler called his paintings 'symphonies' in colour, in protest against the habit of looking at a picture primarily with the intent to discover what it represents; and he applied to Painting the maxim 'Art for Art's sake', which Théophile Gautier had coined for Poetry. Since then the problem of form as against content has been debated. All aims inspired by

[1] The Romantic movement in France was led by the writer and poet Victor Hugo and by the painters Théodore Géricault and Eugéne Delacroix against the followers of Racine and David. Victor Hugo in his famous preface to *Cromwell* (1827) protested against the enforcement in dramatic poetry of the unities of time and of place which he called pseudo-Aristotelian. They seem indeed to be more applicable to painting than to poetry. Compare p. 40.

ulterior motives have been questioned in search for 'purity'; and the means have more and more become ends in themselves. Finally the modern 'abstract', non-objective movements went so far as to repudiate the representation of nature. Painting was to terminate its friendship with both Science and Poetry and to espouse Music.

When Leonardo rebuked Poetry for its extraneous subject-matter, and confessed that this was also a weakness of Painting, he was aware that art had a realm of its own (p. 80, Trat. 32).[1] His subjects, however, were for the most part determined for him, and it never occurred to him to inquire what art was for. In his work the appeal made through its content is not less impressive than its form, one being effectively interpreted by the other. His figures are alive with feeling; they are studied from nature, and they are at the same time integral parts of a pictorial harmony.[2] The Renaissance successfully achieved the fusion of these various elements in a way of its own, while the art movements of the post-Renaissance periods were prone to accentuate one or the other of them. Instead of blending, they confronted them as antitheses. The pendulum swung from Baroque towards classicism; from cold formalism back towards sentimental romanticism; from naturalism and realism back towards abstraction, symbolism, expressionism, surrealism in search for an effective balance; though individual artists did not necessarily belong to one or the other movement exclusively.

c. THE EYE AND THE EAR

Les mots et les couleurs ne sont choses pareilles,
Ni les yeux ne sont des oreilles.—LA FONTAINE.

While Leonardo was taking the lead in the development of Painting as an expression of inner life, he was aware that his art can only convey operations of the mind provided they are of a kind that can be expressed in bodily movement (p. 57, Trat. 19). Painting is confined to motives

---

[1] The following quotations from recent writers are on the same theme: 'Nous croyons à l'autonomie de l'art; l'art pour nous ne pas moyen mais le but' (T. Gautier, *L'Artiste*, 1856); 'I saw that Swinburne in one way, Browning in another, and Tennyson in a third had filled their work with impurities, curiosities about politics, about science, about history, about religion; and that we must create once more the pure work' (W. B. Yeats, *Autobiographies*).

[2] 'Once more I see the *Gioconda*. What voluptuousness in the happy convention. . . . The blue arabesques of the background with their penetrating and caressive rhythm are an enchanting accompaniment to the orange coloured theme—akin to the seduction of the violins in the ouverture of Tannhäuser' (Maurice Denis, 1890).

that can be conveyed through the sense of sight; whereas Poetry can express thoughts that are invisible. The eye and the ear are like windows, by which nature may be perceived in diverse ways.

The difference between the two arts owing to their appeal through different senses was already implied in that ancient saying attributed to Simonides that Poetry was speaking Painting, and Painting mute Poetry. Leonardo took exception to Painting being called mute, since Poetry might then be called blind, but he accepted the differentiation of the sensuous appeals (pp. 55, 58, 67, Trat. 19, 20, 26).

The difference in the means of communication affected the choice of subjects. Poetry in evoking an image has to do so by means of printed or spoken words which are not the things for which they stand. 'Poetry puts down the subjects in imaginary written characters, while Painting puts down the identical reflections that the eye receives as if they were real' (p. 49, Trat. 2). Since the eye can see the object itself, and the ear can only hear its descriptions, Painting is superior in the imitation of the visible world. 'What poet can represent to you in words, oh lover, the true image of your ideal as faithfully as the painter will do? Who will show you the courses of rivers, forests, valleys, and fields . . . with more truth than the painter?' (p. 52, Trat. 18). It seemed obvious to him that here poets cannot compete.

Poetry, on the other hand, is able to describe the working of the mind. 'The domain of Poetry is moral philosophy, that of Painting, natural philosophy' (p. 57, Trat. 19). That is to say, the physical aspect of the world was the special domain of Painting, and thought that of Poetry.

'The true function of the poet is to invent the words of people conversing with one another, only then can he transmit through the sense of hearing an equivalent of nature; for the words created by the human voice are natural phenomena in themselves' (p. 51, Trat. 15). They are sounds and resemble the notes of music.

While the poets' words can only be understood by those people who speak their language, painters are universally understood. 'Now tell me which comes nearer the actual man: the name of the man or his image? The name changes with change of country, but his form is unchanged except by death' (p. 55, Trat. 19).[1]

[1] These thoughts found echoes at the distance of centuries: 'Colours speak all languages, but words are understood only by such a people or nation' (Joseph Addison, Spectator, 416, 1712). 'The advantage which Painting possesses over Poesie is this: that amongst so great a diversity of languages, she makes herself understood to all nations of the world'

d. THE PAINTING POET

'A poem is like a picture'—HORACE.

The difference in approach due to the appeal through two different senses affected not only the choice of subjects, making one art more suitable for rendering the thoughts of men, and the other for depicting visible realities; it also entailed the perception of a different kind of beauty. In Painting the grace of a figure, for instance, depends on the harmony of its proportions; and these had to be shown simultaneously for the relationship to tell. In Poetry a theme was developed in succession, set in measures of time.

Leonardo observed that the poet could only describe outward appearances piecemeal, as if a face were to be revealed bit by bit with the part previously shown covered up. He was unable to render harmonious proportions, which can only be gauged when seen together as a unity (pp. 59, 60, 68, 78, Trat. 21, 22, 27, 32).

Leonardo was in advance of his time. The general tendency of art criticism in the following century was to identify the aims and functions of the two arts rather than to differentiate between them. While painters continued to emulate poets in the expression of the inner life and in the representation of historical events, poets vied with painters in the description of the visible world. They were anxious to show what they could do in a field where their rivals were achieving such spectacular successes. Francisco de Hollanda exclaims: 'It would seem indeed that poets had no other aim than to teach the excellence of painting since one thing of which they are most studious is to paint well and imitate good painting' (*Dialogues*, 1538).

Capriano claimed that Poetry possessed all the faculties and powers of the other arts, being able to imitate anything, for example the form of a lion, its colour, its ferocity, its roar. He divided poets into two classes: moral poets, who give lessons, and natural poets, who describe the scenes of nature (*Della Vera Poetica*).

(John Dryden, *Parallel between Painting and Poetry*, commentary to Charles Du Fresnoy's *De Arte Graphica*, 1716). The Abbé du Bos asserted that the *signes naturels* of painting had a more powerful effect than the *signes artificiels* of poetry because they appealed to the sense of sight, and that therefore a drama enacted on the stage and seen by the eye was the most moving form of poetry (*Réflexions critiques sur la poésie et sur la peinture*, 1719). 'Le littérateur s'exprime avec des abstractions tandis que le peintre concrète au moyen du dessin et de la couleur ses sensations et ses perceptions' (Cézanne).

Carlo Ridolfi relates how Titian while painting for Duke Alfonso d'Este in Ferrara was being visited by Ariosto, who read out to him 'his divine poem' which he was still in the course of writing. The poet derived much advantage from Titian's advice, which helped him in the description of landscapes and 'in setting forth the beauty of Alcina . . .' Ridolfi adds that on this occasion the mute poet and the painter eloquent, 'the Apelles and Homer of those days', had combined (*Le Meraviglie dell' Arte*, 1648).

But Ariosto had to admit in his *Orlando Furioso* that painters could better than he represent the beauty of his fairy Alcina.

> Di persona era tanto ben formata
> Quanto ne finger san pittor industri.   (vii. 11)

He nevertheless proceeded to describe the beauty of her figure. No doubt he was tempted with Titian's help to try his power on a subject which in his times as in those of classical antiquity was considered the highest expression of formal beauty. His description was deemed so successful that the humanist critic Lodovico Dolce, who in his youth had published a translation of Horace's *Ars Poetica*, exhorted artists to take Alcina as their model: 'If painters want without trouble to find a perfect example of a beautiful woman let them read the verses where Ariosto so marvellously describes the beauty of the fairy Alcina, and they will see how good poets are likewise painters' (*Dialogo della Pittura*, 1557).

A few voices, however, were raised in protest. Benedetto Varchi, the Florentine poet and historian, tried to ascribe a separate province to each art. Painting imitates *il di fuori*—the outside world. Poetry chiefly imitates *il di dentro*—the world within (*Due Lezioni*, 1549).

Lodovico Castelvetro restricted the painter's activity to realistic portraiture, and the poet's to the giving of pleasure (*Poetica d'Aristotele*, 1570).

But these were isolated voices. Leonardo's fundamental distinctions between the two arts were not systematically reaffirmed until Lessing assigned to each art its proper boundaries. He, too, was in revolt against a school of pictorial poets that was flourishing during his time. 'Painting by means of form and colour renders objects in space. Poetry by articulate sounds describes actions taking place in the course of time.' He challenged Dolce's above-mentioned recommendation to painters that they should study Ariosto's description of a beautiful woman.

'I recommend it to all poets as a most instructive warning not to try where Ariosto failed.'

'The beauty of a body arises from the harmonious effect produced when the various parts are viewed simultaneously. These parts must, therefore, be situated side by side; and as things situated side by side are the especial concern of painting, it alone can imitate the beauty of the body. The poet who would only be able to describe the component parts of beauty one after another therefore misses completely the representation of formal beauty as such. He feels that these elements, when arranged one after another cannot possibly produce the same effect as when placed side by side' (*Laokoon*, xvi, xx).

Trat. 2]

17

ESEMPIO ET DIFFERENZA TRA PITTURA ET POESIA

SIMILARITY AND DIFFERENCE BETWEEN PAINTING AND POETRY

Tal proportione è dalla immaginatione al' effetto, qual' è dal' ombra al corpo ombroso, e la medesima proportione è dalla poesia alla pittura. perchè la poesia pon' le sue cose nell' immaginatione de lettere, e la pittura le da realmente fori del occhio, dal qual occhio riceve le similitudini non altrimente che s'elle fussino naturali; e la poesia le da sanza essa similitudine, e non passano all' impressiva per la via della virtù visiva come la pittura.

The imagination is to reality as the shadow to the body that casts it and as poetry is to painting, because poetry puts down her subjects in imaginary written characters, while painting puts down the identical reflections that the eye receives, as if they were real, and poetry does not give the actual likeness of things, and does not, like painting, impress the consciousness through the organ of sight.

Trat. 15]

18

ESEMPIO TRA LA POESIA E LA PITTURA

A COMPARISON BETWEEN POETRY AND PAINTING

Non uede l'immaginatione cotal eccellentia, qual uede l'occhio, perchè l'occhio riceue le spetie, ouero similitudini de li obietti e dalli alla impressiua e da essa impressiua al senso comune et li è giudicata, ma la immaginatione non esce fuori da esso senso comune, se non in quanto essa ua alla memoria, e li si ferma e muore, se la cosa immaginata non è di molta eccellentia. et in questo caso si troua la poesia nella mente ouero immaginatiua del poeta, il quale finge le medesime cose del pittore, per le quali fintioni egli uole equipararsi a esso

The imagination cannot visualize such beauty as is seen by the eye, because the eye receives the actual semblances or images of objects and transmits them through the sense organ to the understanding where they are judged. But the imagination never gets outside the understanding (sensus communis);[1] it reaches the memory and stops and dies there if the imagined object is not of great beauty; thus poetry is born in the mind or rather in the imagination of the poet who, because he describes the same things as the painter, claims to be the painter's

[1] See p. 20.

H

pittore, ma in uero ei n'è molto remoto, come di sopra è dimostrato. Adonque in tal caso di fintione diremo con uerità esser tal proportione dalla scientia della pittura alla poesia, qual è dal corpo alla sua ombra deriuatiua, et anchora maggiore proportione, conciosiachè l'ombra di tal corpo almeno entra per l'occhio al senso comune, ma la immaginatione di tale corpo non entra in esso senso, ma li nasce, nell' occhio tenebroso.[1] o, che diferentia è a immaginare tal luce in occhio tenebroso al uederla in atto fuori delle tenebre.

Se tu, poeta, figurerai la sanguinosa battaglia, si sta con la oscura e tenebrosa aria, mediante il fumo delle spauenteuoli et mortali macchine, miste con la spessa poluere intorbidatrice dell' aria, e la paurosa fuga delli miseri spauentati dalla horribile morte. In questo caso il pittore ti supera, perchè la tua penna fia consumata, inanzi che tu descriua a' pieno quel, che immediate il pittore ti rapresenta con la sua scientia.

Et la tua lingua sarà impedita dalla sete, et il corpo dal sonno e fame, prima che tu con parole dimostri quello, che in un istante il pittore ti dimostra. Nella qual pittura non mancha altro, che l'anima delle cose finte, et in ciascun corpo è l'integrità di quella parte, che per un solo aspetto puo dimostrarsi, il che longa et tediosissima cosa sarebbe alla poesia a ridire tutti li mouimenti delli operatori di tal guerra, e le parti delle membra, e lor' ornamenti, delle quali cose la pittura finita con gran' breuità e uerità ti pone innanzi, et a questa tal dimostratione non mancha, se non il romore delle machine, et le grida delli spauentanti uincitori et le grida e pianti delli spauentati, le quali cose anchora il poeta no' po rapresentare al senso del audito. diremo adonque la poesia essere scientia, che sommamente opera nelli

equal! But in truth he is far removed, as has been shown above. Therefore, in regard to imitation, it is true to say that the science of painting stands to poetry in the same relation as a body to its cast shadow; but the difference is even greater; because a shadow penetrates through the eye to the understanding while the object of the imagination does not come from without but is born in the darkness of the mind's eye. What a difference between forming a mental image of such light in the darkness of the mind's eye and actually perceiving it outside the darkness!

If you, poet, had to represent a murderous battle you would have to describe the air obscured and darkened by fumes from frightful and deadly engines mixed with thick clouds of dust polluting the atmosphere, and the panicky flight of wretches fearful of horrible death. In that case the painter will be your superior, because your pen will be worn out before you can fully describe what the painter can demonstrate forthwith by the aid of his science, and your tongue will be parched with thirst and your body overcome by sleep and hunger before you can describe with words what a painter is able to show you in an instant. In his picture only the soul is wanting; each figure is represented so as to show completely that part which faces the given direction. What long and tedious work it would be for poetry to describe all the movements of the fighters in such a battle and the actions of their limbs and their ornaments. This is accomplished with great directness and truth in painting and placed before you, and in such a picture only the sound of the engines, the shouts of the terrifying victors, and the cries and wailing of the terrified victims are wanting, and neither can the poet convey these to the sense of hearing.

It may be said, therefore, that poetry is the science for the blind and painting

[1] See p. 20.

orbi, et la pittura far il medesimo nelli sordi. ma tanto resta più degna la pittura, quanto ella serue a miglior senso.

Solo il uero uffitio del poeta è fingere parole di gente, ch'en sieme parlino, e sol' queste rapresenta al senso del audito tanto, come naturali, perchè in se sono naturali create dall' humana uoce. e' in tutte l'altre consequentie è superato dal pittore.

Ma molto più sanza comparatione son le uarietà, in che s'estende la pittura, che quelle, in che s'estende le parole, perchè infinite cose farà il pittore, che le parole non le potra nominare, per non hauer uocaboli appropriati a quelle. hor non uedi tu, che se 'l pittore vol fingere animali, o' diauoli nel inferno, con quanta abbondanza d'inuentione egli trascorre?

for the deaf. But painting is nobler than poetry inasmuch as it serves the nobler sense.

The only true office of the poet is to invent the words of people who are conversing together—only then can he transmit to the sense of hearing an equivalent of nature, for the words created by the human voice are natural phenomena in themselves.

But in everything else he is outstripped by the painter. The many-sidedness which painting commands is incomparably greater than can be attained by words because the painter can express an infinite variety of things which words cannot describe for want of appropriate terms. Now do you not see to what an abundance of inventions the painter may resort if he wishes to portray animals or devils in hell?[1]

Trat. 13]

19

COME IL PITTORE È SIGNORE D'OGNI SORTE DI GENTE E DI TUTTE LE COSE

THE PAINTER IS LORD OF ALL TYPES OF PEOPLE AND OF ALL THINGS

Sel pittore vol vedere bellezze, che lo innamorino, egli n'è signore di generarle, et se vol vedere cose mostruose, che spaventino, o che sieno bufonesche, e risibili o veramente compassionevoli, ei n'è signore et dio (creatore). e se vol generare siti e deserti, lochi ombrosi o' foschi (freschi) ne' tempi caldi, esso li figura, e cosi lochi caldi ne' tempi freddi. se vol valli (al simile), se vole delle alte cime de' monti scoprire gran campagne, et se vole dopo quelle uedere l'orizzonte del mare, egli n'è signore, e se delle basse

If the painter wishes to see beauties that charm him it lies in his power to create them, and if he wishes to see monstrosities that are frightful, buffoonish, or ridiculous, or pitiable, he can be lord and God (creator) thereof; and if he wishes to produce inhabited regions or deserts, or dark and shady (cool) retreats from the heat, or warm places for cold weather, he can do so. If he wants valleys (likewise) if he wants from high mountain tops to unfold a great plain extending down to the sea's horizon, he is lord to do so; and likewise if from low plains he wishes to see high

[1] For Leonardo's drawings of fantastic animals see drawings of dragons at Windsor, Royal Library, and Plate VI. Compare Lomazzo, *Trattato dell' Arte di Pittura*, book ii, ch. 20: 'Dipinse un drago in zuffa con un Leone con tant' arte, che mette in dubbio chiunque lo riguarda chi di loro debba restare vittorioso; tanto espresse egli in ciascuno i moti difensivi ed offensivi', and ibid., book vi, ch. 20: 'Riferi Francesco Melzi che Leonardo fece un drago che combatteva con un leone, cosa molto mirabile a vedere.' Compare also Vasari, ed. Milanesi, iv, pp. 23–4, and the copy of a Leonardo drawing in the Uffizi reproduced in Suida, *Leonardo und sein Kreis*, fig. 117.

ualli vol uedere gli alti monti, o' delli alti monti le basse ualli e spiaggie. et in effetto, ciò, ch'è nel' uniuerso per essentia, presentia o' immaginatione, esso l' ha prima nella mente, e poi nelle mani; e quelle sono di tanta eccellentia, che in pari tempo generano una proportionata armonia in un' solo sguardo, qual' fanno le cose.

mountains, or from high mountains low plains and the sea shore. In fact, whatever exists in the universe, in essence, in appearance, in the imagination, the painter has first in his mind and then in his hands; and these are of such excellence that they are able to present a proportioned and harmonious view of the whole that can be seen simultaneously, at one glance, just as things in nature.

Trat. 46]   20

DE PITTURA E POESIA

Per fingere parole la poesia supera la pittura, et per fingere fatti la pittura supera la poesia, et quella proportione che' da' fatti alle parole, tal' è dalla pittura ad essa poesia, perchè i fatti sono subbieto dell' occhio, et le parole subbieto dell' orecchio, et cosi li sensi hanno la medesima proportione infra loro, quale hanno li loro obbieti infra se medesimi, et per questo giudico la pittura essere superiore alla poesia. Ma per non sapere li suoi operatori dire la sua ragione è restata lungo tempo sanza aduocati. Perchè lei non parla, ma per se si dimostra e termina ne' fatti; et la poesia finisce in parole, co' le quali come briosa se stessa lauda.

ON PAINTING AND POETRY

Poetry is superior to painting in the presentation of words, and painting is superior to poetry in the presentation of facts. And painting is to poetry in the same relation as facts are to words. Since facts are subject to the eye and words are subject to the ear, the relation which these senses have to one another also exists between their respective objects. For this reason I judge painting to be superior to poetry. But as painters did not know how to plead for their own art she was left without advocates for a long time. For painting does not talk; but reveals herself as she is, ending in reality; and Poetry ends in words in which she eloquently sings her own praises.

Trat. 18]   21

PITTORE, CHE DISPUTA COL POETA

Qual poeta con parole ti mettera in' anzi, o amante, la uera effiggie della tua iddea con tanta uerità, qual farà il pittore? quale fia quello, che ti dimostrera siti de' fiumi, boschi, ualli et campagne, doue si rapresenti li tuoi passati piaceri con più uerità chel pittore? e se tu dici che la pittura è una poesia muta per se, se non u'è, chi dica o parli per lei quello che la rapresenta, or non uedi tu, chel tuo libro si troua in peggiore grado? perchè anchora ch'egli habbia un homo, che parli per lui, non si uede niente della cosa, di

THE PAINTER'S DISPUTE WITH THE POET

What poet can represent to you in words, oh lover, the true image of your ideal as faithfully as the painter will do? Who can show you the courses of rivers, the forests, valleys, and fields, and call up memories of past pleasures therein with more truth than the painter?

And if you say: painting is poetry, which in itself is mute unless there is some one to expound it and explain what it represents, do you not see that your book is worse off because even if there is a man to expound it, one cannot see anything of what he is saying, while he who

che si parla come si uederà di quello, che parla per le pitture; le quali pitture, se saranno ben proportionati li atti con li loro accidenti mentali, saranno intese, come se parlassino.

speaks of pictures will speak of things that can be seen; and these pictures will be understood as if they could speak, if the actions of the figures are well attuned to their states of mind.

Trat. 14] 22

DEL POETA E DEL PITTORE

La pittura serve a più degno senso, che la poesia, e fa con più verità le figure delle opere di natura ch'il poeta; e sono molto più degne l'opere di natura chelle parole, che sono l'opera dell' homo, perche tal proportione è da l'opere delli homini a' quelle della natura, qual è quella, ch'è dal homo a dio. Adonque è più degna cosa l'imitare le cose di natura, che sono le vere similitudini in fatto, che con parole imitare li fatti e parole degli homini. e se tu, poeta, uoi descrivere l'opere de natura co' la tua semplice professione, fingendo diversi siti e forme di varie cose, tu sei superato dal pittore con infinita proportione di potentia; ma se vuoi uestirti de l'altrui scientie separate da essa poesia, elle non sono tue, come Astrologia, Rettorica, Teologia, Filosofia, Geometria, Aritmetica e simili, tu non sei allora poeta, tu ti trasmuti, e non sei più quello, di che qui si parla. hor non uedi tu, che se tu uoi andare alla natura che tu ui uai con mezzi di scientie fatte d'altrui sopra gli effetti di natura? et il pittore per se, sanza ajuto di scientiali ò d'altri mezzi ua immediate alla imitatione d'esse opere di natura. con questa si mouono li amanti uerso li simulacri della cosa amata, à parlare colle imitate

THE POET AND THE PAINTER

Painting serves a nobler sense than poetry and represents the works of nature with more truth than the poet. The works of nature are much nobler than speech which was invented by man; for the works of man are to the works of nature as man is to God. Therefore, it is a nobler profession to imitate the things of nature which are the true and actual likenesses than to imitate in words the actions and speeches of men. And if you, poet, wish to confine yourself exclusively to your own profession in describing the works of nature, representing diverse places and forms of various objects, you will be out-distanced by the painter's infinitely greater power. But if you clothe yourself in other sciences that are outside the realm of poetry and are not yours, such as astronomy, rhetoric, theology, philosophy, geometry, arithmetic, and so forth, then you are no longer a poet. You have changed into something else and no longer enter into the present consideration. Do you not see that in describing nature you do so with the aid of sciences made by others, while the painter proceeds unaided and without drawing on scientific or other aids straight to the imitation of the same works of nature.

Thereby lovers are made to turn to the portraits of their beloved, to speak to the painting which represents them.[1]

[1] Compare Baldassare Castiglione's poem on his portrait by Raphael, now in the Louvre. His wife is supposed to be writing to him during his absence:
'When alone the portrait by Raphael's hand
Recalls your face and relieves my cares,
I play with it and laugh with it and joke,
I speak to it and as though it could reply,

It often seems to me to nod and motion,
To want to say something and speak your words,
Your boy knows and greets his father babbling,
Herewith I am consoled and beguile the long days.'

pitture; con questa si mouono li popoli con inferuorati uoti a ricercare li simulacri delli iddii; et non un uedere le opere de' poeti, che con parole figurino li medesimi idii; con questa s'ingannano li animali. già uid' io una pittura, che ingannaua il cane mediante la similitudine del suo patrone, alla quale esso cane facea grandissima festa; e similmente ho uisto i cani baiare et uoler mordere i cani dipinti; et una scimmia far infinite pazzie contro ad un' altra scimmia dipinta. ho ueduto le rondini uolare e possarsi sopra li ferri dipinti, che sportano fori delle finestre delli edifitii.

Thereby the peoples are stirred with fervent vows to seek out the images of the Gods (but this does not apply to the works of poets who describe the same gods with words); thereby are animals deceived. I once saw a dog, deceived by a portrait or his master, giving him a joyful welcome; and I have observed dogs barking and trying to bite dogs represented in a painting; and I saw a monkey indulging in endless pranks with another monkey represented in a painting. I have seen swallows fly to perch on iron bars painted in imitation of lattices that protrude from the windows of buildings.[1]

Trat. 19]   23

COME LA PITTURA AUANZA TUTTE L'OPERE HUMANE PER SOTILE SPECULATIONE APPARTENENTI A QUELLA

HOW PAINTING SURPASSES ALL WORKS OF MEN BY THE SUBTLE SPECULATIONS CONNECTED WITH IT

L'occhio, che si dice finestra dell' anima, è la principal uia, donde il comune senso pò più copiosa et magnificamente considerare l'infinite opere di natura, et l'orecchio è 'l secondo, il quale si fa nobile per le cose raconte, le quali ha ueduto l'occhio. se uoi Istoriograffi, ò poeti, ò altri matematici non hauestiue con l'occhio uisto le cose, male le potreste uoi rifferire per le scritture. et se tu, poeta, figurerai una istoria, con la pittura della penna, il pittore col penello la farà

The eye, which is the window of the soul, is the chief organ whereby the understanding can have the most complete and magnificent view of the infinite works of nature; and the ear comes second, which acquires dignity by hearing the things the eye has seen.[2] If you historians, or poets, or mathematicians, had never seen things with your eyes, you could report but imperfectly on them in your writing. And if you, oh poet, tell a story with your pen, the

[1] The Greek painter Zeuxis is said to have painted grapes so lifelike that birds pecked at them (Plinius, *Historia Naturalis*, book xxxv, ch. 65).

The history of Greek painting abounds in anecdotes about works by famous artists which produced the illusion on the spectator that he was looking at nature itself. For the first time in history such works were being produced, and the public, never having seen anything like them, considered them marvellous. Leonardo, in order to drive home his argument and to show what art could achieve, tells similar incidents of lifelike paintings which he himself must have looked upon as curiosities (Trat. 19, 25. Compare Vasari's anecdote of Donatello at work on the Zuc-

cone: 'mentre che lo lavorava, guardandolo, tuttavia gli diceva: favella, favella', ii. 405.)

A man as well versed in matters of art as Fra Luca Pacioli, who was on terms of personal friendship with Piero della Francesca, Leon Battista Alberti, and Leonardo, compared the lifelike quality of the figures in Leonardo's Last Supper with the grapes of Zeuxis and with the veil painted by Parrhasios which Zeuxis tried to draw aside (*De Divina Proportione*, iii); and Leonardo's portrait of Ginevra di Amerigho Benci is described in the *Libro di Antonio Billi* (ed. C. Frey, 1892, p. 51) as: 'tanto bene finita, che ella propria non era altrimenti'.

[2] Compare Horace, *Ars Poetica*, 180 f.

di più facile sattisfatione et meno tediosa ad essere compresa. se tu dimanderai la pittura mutta poesia, anchora il pittore potra dire la poesia orba pittura.

Hor guarda, quale è più dannoso mostro, ol cieco, ol mutto? se 'l poeta è libero come 'l pittore nelle inuentioni, le sue fintioni non sonno di tanta satisfatione alli homini, quanto le pitture; perche, se la poesia s'estende con le parolle a figurare forme, atti e siti, il pittore si moue con le proprie similitudini delle forme a contrafare esse forme.

Hor guarda, qual' è più propinquo al homo, ol nome de homo, o la similitudine d'esso homo? il nome del homo si uaria in uarij paesi, et la forma non è mutata, se non per morte. e se il poeta serue al senso per la uia del' orecchio, il pittore per la uia del' occhio, più degno senso. ma io non uoglio da questi tali altro, che uno bono pittore, che figuri 'l furore d'una battaglia, e che 'l poeta ne scriui un' altra, e che sieno messi in pubblico di compagnia. Uedrai, doue più si

painter with his brush can tell it more easily, with simpler completeness, and so that it is less tedious to follow. And if you call painting dumb poetry, the painter may call poetry blind painting.[1]

Now which is the more grievous affliction, to be blind or to be dumb?

Though the poet is as free to invent,[2] as the painter, his fictions do not give so great a satisfaction to men as painting, for though poetry is able to describe forms, actions, and places in words, the painter employs the exact images of the forms and represents them as they are. Now tell me which comes nearer to the actual man: the name of the man or the image of the man: the name of the man changes with change of country; but his form is unchanged except by death.

And if the poet gratifies the understanding by way of the ear, the painter does so by the eye, the nobler sense. But I shall ask no more than that a good painter should represent the fury of a battle and that the poet should describe one and that both these battles be put before the public. You will soon see

[1] The antithesis of Simonides of Keos ran thus: 'Painting is dumb poetry, and poetry is speaking painting' (quoted by Plutarch, *De Gloria Atheniensium*, ch. 3). Leonardo protests against his art being called dumb; rather should poetry be called invisible or blind. Francesco d'Hollanda also protests: 'That poets should call painting dumb poetry only implies that they were unskilled in painting, for had they realized how much more she speaks and sets forth than her sister they would not have said it, and I will rather maintain that poetry is the dumb art' (Dialogo II).

[2] Cennino Cennini (*Libro dell' Arte*, i) claimed a seat for Painting with Poetry among the Liberal Arts on the same ground: 'È un arte che si chiama dipingere che conviene avere fantasia e operazione di mano, di trovare cose non vedute cacciandosi sotto ombre di naturali, e fermarle, con la mano, dando a dimostrare quello che non è sia. È con ragione merita metterla a sedere in secondo grado alla scienza e coronarla di poesia.' And

he compares the poet, who is free to compose and join together as he pleases, to the painter who constructs a figure half-man and half-horse according to his fancy.

Freedom of imagination in the representation of things that do not exist and actions that never took place was conceded to both poets and painters in Horace's *Ars Poetica* (c. 9–10: 'Pictoribus atque poetis quidlibet audendi semper fuit aequa potestas'). This principle may be traced back to Aristotle (*Poetics*, 25), who said that both poet and painter represented things by imitation, and that there were three ways of doing this: things may be imitated as they are, or as they appear to be, or as they should be, 'we concede this freedom to the poets'. Philostratus the Younger (Εἰκόνες, Prœmium) says: 'If one reflects upon the matter, the art of painting has a certain kinship with poetry, and that an element of imagination is common to them both.'

fermeranno li ueditori, doue più considereranno, doue si darà più laude, et quale satisfarà meglio. certo la pittura di gran longa più uttile et bella più piacerà. poni in scritto il nome d'iddio in un locho, e ponui la sua figura a riscontro, uedrai, quale fia più riuerita.

Se la pittura abbraccia in se tutte le forme della natura, uoi non hauete se non li nomi, li quali non sono universali come le forme. se voi hauete li effetti delle dimostrationi, noi habbiamo le dimostrationi delli effetti.

Tolgasi un poeta, che descriva le bellezze d'una donna al suo inamorato, e tolgasi un pittore, che la figuri, vedrassi, doue la natura volgerà più il giudicatore inamorato. certo, il cimento delle cose dovrebbe lasciare dar' la sententia alla sperientia, uoi hauete messa la pittura fra l'arti mechaniche. certo, se i pittori fussero atti a laudare col scrivere l'opere loro, come uoi, creddo non giacerebbe in cosi vile cognome. se uoi la chiamate mechanicha, perchè è prima manuale, che le mani figurano quello, che trovano nella fantasia, uoi scrittori, dissegnando con la penna manualmente quello, che nello ingegno uostro si trova, e se uoi diceste essere mechanicha, perchè si fa a prezzo, chi cade in questo errore, s'errore pò chiamarsi, più di uoi? se uoi leggete per li studi, non andate da chi più vi premia? fate uoi alchuna opera senza qualche premio? benchè questo non

which will draw more of the spectators and where there will be more discussion, to which more praise will be given, and which will satisfy the more. Undoubtedly the painting, being by far the more intelligible and beautiful, will please most. Inscribe the name of God in any place and set up His image opposite and you will see which will be more revered.

Painting embraces within itself all the forms of nature, while you have nothing but their names which are not universal as form is; and if you have the effects of demonstrations we have demonstrations of the effects. Take the case of a poet who describes the beauty of a lady to her lover and a painter who portrays her and you will see where nature will lead the enamoured judge.

Certainly the proof should be allowed to rest on the verdict of experience. You have set painting among the mechanical arts, but truly, were painters as ready equipped as you are to praise their own works in writing, I doubt whether it would endure the stigma of so base a name. If you call it mechanical[1] because it is by manual work that the hands design what is in the imagination—you writers set down with the pen by manual work what originates in your mind.

And if you call it mechanical because it is done for money, who fall into this error—if error it can be called—more than you yourselves? If you lecture for instruction, do you not go to whoever pays you most?[2] Do you do any work without pay? And yet I do not say this

---

[1] See p. 12.

[2] Compare the behaviour of the crowds of poets who flocked to the papal court of Leo X (L. Pastor, *Geschichte der Päpste*, vol. iv. i, parts 10, 11): 'Leo X distributed his favours on all sides; he gave indiscriminately to the learned, to true poets and happy improvisators, to poetasters and second-rate clowns. The more he gave, the more greedy the poets, who were dissatisfied unless the pope asked them frequently to meals, made them recite at church festivals and allowed free entry at dinner time every day; the shameless crowd of poets soon followed the pope everywhere, he was not even safe in his bedroom. . . . In spite of his liberality Leo X could not satisfy everybody. With his growing financial difficulties complaints grew louder. . . . Among his accusers was the poet who deemed ancient poets happier for the sole reason that they had a greater Maecenas. . . .'

dico per biasimare simili opinioni, perchè ogni fatica aspetta premio. e potrà dire un poeta: io farò una fintione che significava cose grande; questo medesimo farà il pittore, come fece Apelle la calunnia. se uoi dicesti, la poesia è più eterna, per questo dirò essere piu eterne l'opere dun calderaio. chel tempo piu le conserva, che le vostre o' nostre opere, niente dimeno è di poca fantasia; e la pittura si può, depingendo sopra rame con colori di vetro, farla molto più etterna. noi per arte possiamo esser detti nipoti à dio. s'ella poesia s'estende in filosofia morale, e questa in filosofia naturale; se quella descrive l'operationi della mente, che considera quella, se la mente opera nei movimenti. se quella spaventa i populi con le infernali fintioni, questa con le medesime cose in atto fa il simile, pongasi il poeta a figurare una bellezza, una fierezza, una cosa nefand' e brutta, una mostruosa col pittore, faccia a suo modo, come uole, trasmutatione di forme, che il pittore non sattisfaccia più. no s'egli visto pitture avere havuto tanta conformità con la cosa imitata, che hanno ingannato homini et animali?

in blame of such views for every form of labour looks for its reward. And if a poet should say: I will write a story which signifies great things, the painter can do likewise, for even so Apelles painted the Calumny.[1] If you were to say that poetry is more lasting,[2] I say the works of a coppersmith are more lasting still, for time preserves them longer than your works or ours; nevertheless they display little imagination. And a picture can be made more enduring by painting upon copper in enamel colours. We by our art may be called the grandchildren of God.[3] If poetry treats of moral philosophy, painting has to do with natural philosophy.[4] If poetry describes the working of the mind, painting considers the working of the mind as reflected in the movements (of the body).[5] If poetry can terrify people by fictions of hell,[6] painting can do as much by placing the same things before the eye. Suppose the poet as against the painter sets himself to represent some image of beauty or terror, or a base, ugly, monstrous thing, whatever variety of forms he may in his way produce, the painter will satisfy the more. Have we not seen pictures so closely resembling the actual thing that they deceived both men and beasts?[7]

[1] See Lucian, 'Slander', a warning, for the description of Apelles' picture which inspired Renaissance artists to paint and engrave the same subject. Botticelli's version is one of his masterpieces. Mantegna's drawing was copied by Rembrandt.

[2] See p. 93.

[3] See Dante, *Inferno*, xi. 105.

[4] Leonardo follows the Latin tradition of connecting poetry with rhetoric, while painting, according to him, is related to the natural sciences. See pp. 12 ff. John Constable in a lecture at the Royal Institution in 1836 asked: 'why may not landscape be considered as a branch of natural philosophy, of which

pictures are but experiments?'

[5] See p. 37.

[6] Like Dante's *Inferno*.

[7] In the bulk of classical writing on Art—whether poetry or painting or sculpture—although the rights of fiction and imagination were safeguarded, the stress was on verisimilitude. Even when imaginary scenes were described or painted, it was thought essential to make them seem credible in the sense that they could be conceived as actually appearing under such forms in physical life. The Renaissance writers on Art took over the point of view of classical literature (compare Trat. 14).

DIFFERENTIA, CHE HA LA PITTURA CON LA POESIA

La pittura è una poesia che si uede e non si sente, e la poesia è una pittura, che si sente e non si vede. adonque queste due poesie, o vuoi dire due pitture, hanno scambiati li sensi, per li quali esse dovrebbono penetrare all' intelletto. perchè se l'una e l'altra dee passare al senso comune[4] per il senso più nobile, cioè l'occhio, et se l'una e l'altra è poesia, esse hanno a passare per il senso meno nobile, cioè l'audito. adonque daremo la pittura al giuditio del sordo nato, et la poesia sarà giudicata dal cieco nato; et se la pittura sarà figurata con li mouimenti appropriati alli accidenti mentali delle figure, che operano in qualonque caso, sanza dubbio il sordo nato intenderà le operationi ed intentioni delli operatori, ma 'l cieco nato non intenderà mai cosa che dimostri 'l poeta, la qual faccia honore a essa poesia, conciosiachè delle nobili sue parti è il figurare li gesti e li componimenti delle istorie e li siti ornati e dilettevoli con le trasparenti acque, per le quali si vede li verdeggianti fondi delli suoi corsi, scherzare l'onde sopra prati e minute giarre con l'erbe, che con lor si mischiano insieme con li sguicianti pesci, et simili discretioni, li quali si potrebbono così dire ad un sasso, come ad un ciecho nato, perche mai vide nissuna cosa, di che si compone la bellezza del mondo, cioè luce, tenebre, colore, corpo, figura, sito, remotione, propinquità, moto e quiete, le quali son dieci ornamenti della natura. ma il sordo, havendo perso il senso meno nobile, anchora ch'egli habbia insieme persa la loquela, perchè mai udì parlare, mai potè imparare alcun linguaggio, ma questo intenderà bene ogni accidente, che sia nelli corpi humani, meglio che un, che parli e che habbia

THE DIFFERENCE BETWEEN PAINTING AND POETRY

Painting is poetry which is seen and not heard, and poetry is a painting which is heard but not seen. These two arts, you may call them both either poetry or painting, have here interchanged the senses by which they penetrate to the intellect. Whatever is painted must pass by the eye, which is the nobler sense, and whatever is poetry must pass through a less noble sense, namely the ear, to the understanding. Therefore, let the painting be judged by a man born deaf, and the poem by one born blind. If in the painting the actions of the figures are in every case expressive of the purpose in their minds, the beholder, though born deaf, is sure to understand what is intended, but the listener born blind will never understand the things the poet describes which reflect honour on the poem, including such important parts as the indication of gestures, the compositions of the stories, the description of beautiful and delightful places with limpid waters through which the green bed of the stream can be seen, and the play of the waves rolling through meadows and over pebbles, mingling with blades of grass and with playful fishes, and similar subtle detail which may as well be addressed to a stone as to a man born blind who never in his life has seen what makes the beauty of the world, namely, light, shade, colour, body, figure, position, distance, nearness, motion, and rest[1]—these ten ornaments of nature. But the deaf man who has lost a sense less noble, even though he may thereby be deprived of speech (for never having heard anybody talk he could not learn any language), will understand all the actions of the human body better than one who can speak and hear, and he

[1] See p. 20.

udito, e similemente conoscerà l'opere de' pittori e quello, che in esse si rapresenti, et a chi tali figure sieno propriate.

will therefore be able to understand the works of painters and recognize the actions of their figures.

Trat. 21]

25

CHE DIFFERENTIA È DALLA PITTURA ALLA POESIA

THE DIFFERENCE BETWEEN PAINTING AND POETRY

La pittura è una poesia muta, et la poesia è una pittura ciecha, e l'una e l'altra va imitando la natura, quanto è possibile alle loro potentie, e per l'una e per l'altra si pò dimostrare molti morali costumi, come fece Apelle con la sua calunnia. ma della pittura, perchè serue al' occhio, senso più nobile, che l'orecchio, obbietto della poesia, ne risulta una proportione armonicha, cioè, che si come di molte uarie uoci insieme aggionte ad un medesimo tempo, ne risulta una proportione armonicha, la quale contenta tanto il senso dello audito, che li auditori restano con stupente ammiratione, quasi semiuiui. ma molto più farà le proportionali bellezze d'un angelico uiso, posto in pittura, della quale proportionalità ne risulta un' armonico concento, il quale serue al' occhio in uno medesimo tempo, che si faccia dalla musica all' orecchio, e se tale armonia delle bellezze sarà mostrata allo amante di quella, da chi tale bellezze sono imitate, sanza dubbio esso resterà con istupenda ammiratione e gaudio incomparabile e superiore a tutti l'altri sensi. Ma della poesia, la qual s'abbia à stendere alla figuratione d'una perfetta bellezza con la figuratione particulare di ciaschuna parte, della quale si compone in pittura la predetta armonia, non ne risulta altra gratia, che si facessi à far sentire nella musicha ciaschuna uoce per se sola in uarj tempi, delle quali non si comporrebbe alcun concento, come se uolessimo mostrare un' uolto à parte à parte, sempre ricoprendo quelle, che prima si mostrano, delle quali dimostrationi l'obliuione non lascia comporre alcuna proportionalità d'armonia, perchè

Painting is mute poetry, and poetry is blind painting. Both aim at imitating nature as closely as lies in their power, and both can be used for expounding divers customs and morals, as Apelles did in his 'Calumny'.

And from painting which serves the eye, the noblest sense, arises harmony of proportions; just as many different voices joined together and singing simultaneously produce a harmonious proportion which gives such satisfaction to the sense of hearing that listeners remain spellbound with admiration as if half alive. But the effect of the beautiful proportion of an angelic face in a painting is much greater, for these proportions produce a harmonious concord which reaches the eye simultaneously, just as (a chord in) music affects the ear; and if this beautiful harmony be shown to the lover of her whose beauties are portrayed, he will without doubt remain spellbound in admiration and in a joy without parallel and superior to all other sensations.

But a poem which aims at the representation of perfect beauty has to describe separately each particular part that makes up the harmony of a picture; and its charm is no greater than that which would arise if in music each voice were to be heard separately at different times without producing any concord, or if a face were to be revealed bit by bit with the part previously shown covered up, so that we are prevented by our forgetfulness from composing any harmony of proportions because the eye cannot

l'occhio non le abbraccia co' la sua uirtù uissiua a' un medesimo tempo. il simile accade nelle bellezze di qualonque cosa finta dal poeta, le quali, per essere le sue parti dette separatamente in separati tempi, la memoria nō ne riceue alcuna armonia.

embrace the whole simultaneously in its field of vision.

The same is the case with all beautiful things described by the poet. They are all revealed in separate parts, and at different times, so that the memory does not receive any harmony therefrom.[1]

Trat. 22] **26**

DIFFERENTIA INFRA POESIA E PITTURA

THE DIFFERENCE BETWEEN POETRY AND PAINTING

La pittura immediate ti si rapresenta con quella dimostratione, per la quale il suo fattore l'a generata, et da quel piacere al senso massimo, qual' dare possa alcuna cosa creata dalla natura. Et in questo caso il poeta, che manda le medesime cose al comun senso per la uia dell' udito, minor senso, non dà al occhio altro piacere, che s'un sentissi raccontare una cosa. Hor uedi, che differentia è dal udire raccontare una cosa, che dà piacere al occhio con lunghezza di tempo, o uederla con quella prestezza, che si uedono le cose naturali. et anchora che le cose de' poeti sieno con longho interuallo di tempo lette, spesse sono le uolte, che le non sonno intese e bisogna farli sopra diuersi comenti, de' quali rarissime uolte tali comentatori intendono, qual' fusse la mente del poeta; e molte uolte li lettori non leggano, se non piccola parte delle loro opere per dissaggio di tempo. Ma l'opera del pittore immediate è compresa dalli suoi risguardatori.

Painting presents the impression which the artist wished to convey all at once and gives as much pleasure to the noblest sense as any work created by nature. But a poet, wishing to convey the same things to the 'sensus communis' through the inferior sense of hearing, gives no more pleasure to the eye than if one were listening to something.

Now look what difference there is between listening for a long time to a tale about something which gives pleasure to the eye and actually seeing it all at once as works of nature are seen. Moreover, the works of poets are read at long intervals; they are often not understood and require many explanations, and commentators very rarely know what was in the poet's mind; often only a small part of the poet's works is read for want of time. But the work of the painter is immediately understood by its beholders.[2]

Trat. 23] **27**

DELLA DIFFERENTIA ET ANCHORA SIMILITUDINE, CHE HA LA PITTURA CO' LA POESIA

OF THE DIFFERENCE AND ALSO THE SIMILARITY WHICH PAINTING HAS WITH POETRY

La pittura ti rapresenta in un' subito la sua essentia nella uirtù uisiua e per il proprio mezzo donde la impressiua riceue li obbietti naturali, et anchora nel mede-

Painting presents its subject to thee in one instant through the sense sight, through the same organ that transmits the natural objects to the mind; and at

---

[1] Proportions were the source of genuine and intense pleasure. A well-proportioned work of art was 'a thing great and divine' to Leon Battista Alberti, and 'a great joy' to

Leonardo, 'superior to anything music or poetry could produce'. Compare p. 72.

[2] Horace, *Ars Poetica*, 180 f.

simo tempo, nel quale si compone l'armonicha proportionalità delle parti, che compongono il tutto, che contenta il senso; e la poesia rifferisce il medesimo, ma con mezzo meno degno che l'occhio, il quale porta nella impressiua più confusamente e con più tardità le figurationi delle cose nominate, che non fa l'occhio, uero mezzo infra l'obbietto e la impressiua, il quale immediate conferisce con somma verità le vere superfitie et figure di quel, che dinnanzi se gli appresenta. delle quali ne nasce la proportionalità detta armonia, che con dolce concento contenta il senso, non altrimente, che si facciano le proportionalità di diverse uoci al senso dello audito, il quale anchora è men degno, che quello dell' occhio, perchè tanto, quanto ne nasce, tanto ne more, et è si veloce nel morire, come nel nascere. il che intervenire non pò nel senso del vedere, perche, se tu rappresenterai all' occhio una bellezza humana composta di proportionalità di belle membra, esse bellezze non sono si mortali nè si presto si struggono, come fa la musica, anzi, ha lunga permanentia e ti si lascia vedere e considerare, e non rinasce, come fa la musica nel molto sonare, nè t'induce fastidio, anzi, t'innamora ed è causa, che tutti li sensi insieme con l'occhio la uorrebbon possedere, e pare, che a garra uogliono combatter con l'occhio. pare, che la bocca se la uorebbe per se in corpo; l'orecchio piglia piacere d'udire le sue bellezze; il senso del tatto la uorrebbe penetrare per tutti gli suoi meati; il naso anchora vorebbe ricevere l'aria, ch'al continuo di lei spira. ma la bellezza di tal armonia il tempo in pochi anni la distrugge, il che non accade in tal bellezza immitata dal pittore, perchè il tempo longamente la conserva; et l'occhio,

the same time the harmonious proportions of the parts composing the whole react and delight the eye. Poetry transmits the same subject through a sense which is less noble and which impresses on the mind the shapes of the objects it describes more slowly and confusedly than the eye, which is the true and direct intermediary between the object and the mind, and which transmits with the greatest accuracy the surfaces and shapes of whatever presents itself. And from these shapes is born the proportionality called harmony, which delights the sense of sight with sweet concord just as the proportions of diverse voices delight the sense of hearing. But the harmony of music is less noble than the harmony which appeals to the eye, because sound dies as soon as it is born, and its death is as swift as its birth, and this cannot happen with the sense of sight. For if you present to the eye the beauty of a human figure composed of fine proportions, these beauties will not be as transient nor will they be destroyed as swiftly as in music. On the contrary, beauty has a long life; it can be enjoyed and examined at leisure without having to be continually reborn like music which has to be played again and again, and it will not weary you; on the contrary, it will inspire you with love and not only the eye but all your senses with a longing for possession; and all the senses will seem to compete with the eye; as if the mouth would like to swallow it bodily, as if the ear took pleasure in listening to the descriptions of its beauty, as if the sense of touch liked to draw it in through all its pores and as if the nose would like to inhale the air which continually breathes from it.

In nature time destroys the beauty of such harmony in a few years; this does not happen to the same beauty imitated by the painter; time will preserve it for a long while. And the eye, exercising its

inquanto al suo uffitio, piglia il vero piacere di tal bellezza dipinta, qual si facessi
nella bellezza viva mancali,[1] il tatto il
qual si fa maggior fratello nel medesimo
tempo, il quale poichè avrà avuto il suo
intento, non impedisce la ragione del
considerare la divina bellezza. et in questo
caso la pittura immitata da quella in gran
parte supplisce, il che supplire non potrà
la discretione del poeta, il quale in questo
caso si uole equiparare al pittore, ma non
s'auede, che le sue parole, nel far men-
tione delle membra di tal bellezza, il
tempo le divide l'un da l'altro, e' infra-
mette l'obliuione et diuide le proportioni, le quali lui sanza gran prolissità non
può nominare; et non potendole nominare, esso non può comporne l'armonicha
proportionalità, la quale è composta de
diuine proportioni. e per questo un
medesimo tempo, nel quale s'include la
speculatione d'una bellezza dipinta, non
può dare una bellezza descritta, e fa
peccato contro natura quel, che si de'e
mettere per l'occhio, a uolerlo mettere
per l'orecchio. lasciaui entrare l'uffitio
della musicha, e non ui mettere la
scientia della pittura, uera imitatrice delle
naturali figure di tutte le cose. Che ti
moue, o homo, ad abbandonare le proprie tue abitationi della cità e lasciare li
parenti et amici, et andare in luoghi
campestri per monti e ualli, se non la
naturale bellezza del mondo, la quale, se
ben consideri, sol col senso del uedere
fruisci? e se il poeta uol in tal caso chiamarsi anchora lui pittore, perchè non
pigliaui tali siti descritti dal poeta e
startene in casa sanza sentire il superchio
callore del sole? o non t'era questo più

function, will take as much pleasure in
the painted beauty as it did in the living
beauty which it has lost; the sense of
touch at the same time is made senior
brother,[2] and as it will have been satisfied
will leave reason unimpeded to the contemplation of the divine beauty.

And in this case the painting can take
the place of the original which is destroyed, while the description of the poet
is not able to do so. The poet who tries
to emulate in this the painter does not
take into account that the words which
he uses to describe the various elements
of beauty are separated from one another
by lapses of time which introduce obli-
vion and sever the proportions. These he
cannot describe without using long
phrases, and he cannot therefore with
words convey the harmonious relation
of the divine proportions. Beauty cannot be described in words in the same
time which it takes to view beauty in a
painting. It is a sin against nature to want
to give to the ear what is meant for the
eye. Let music enter there and do not
try to put in her place the science of
painting, the true imitator of all the
shapes of nature.

What induces you, oh man, to depart
from your home in town, to leave parents
and friends, and go to the country-side
over mountains and valleys, if it is not
the beauty of the world of nature which,
on considering, you can only enjoy
through the sense of sight; and as the
poet in this also wants to compete with
the painter, why do you not take the
poet's descriptions of such landscapes
and stay at home without exposing
yourself to the excessive heat of the sun?
Would that not be more expedient and

---

[1] H. Ludwig introduces a semicolon before
mancagli, but in the manuscript the sign of
punctuation (a comma) is placed after *mancali*,
which changes the sentence; the meaning,
however, remains obscure in either case.
Probably the word *che* or *ma* was left out and

the passage should read *ma mancagli*.

[2] According to Aristotle (*De Anima*) the
sense of touch comes first and can exist without the other four senses; these, on the other
hand, depend on the sense of touch for their
existence.

utile e men faticha, perche si fa al fresco e sanza moto e periculo di malatia? ma l'anima non potea fruire il beneficio de li occhi, finestre delle sue habitationi, e non potea ricevere le spetie de li allegri siti, non potea vedere l'ombrose ualli rigate dallo scherzare delli serpeggianti fiumi, non potea vedere li varj fiori, che con loro colori fanno armonia al' occhio, e cosi tutte l'altre cose, che ad esso occhio rappresentare si possono. ma se 'l pittore nelli freddi e rigidi tempi del' inverno ti pone innanti li medesimi paesi dipinti od altri, ne' quali tu habbi ricevuto li tuoi piaceri apresso a qualche fonte, tu possi rivedere tu, amante, con la tua amata nelli fioriti prati, sotto le dolci ombre delle verdeggianti piante, non riceverai tu altro piacere, che ad udire tal effetto descritto dal poeta?

qui risponde 'l poeta et cede alle sopradette raggioni, ma dice, che supera l' pittore, perche lui fa parlare e raggionare li homini con diverse fintioni, nelle quali ei finge cose, che non sono; e che commouerà li homini a pigliare l'armi; e che descriverà il cielo, le stelle e la natura e l'arti e ogni cosa. al quale si risponde che nissuna di queste cose, di che egli parla, è sua professione propria, ma che, s'ei uole parlare et orare, è da persuadere, che in questo gli è vinto dal' oratore; e se parla d'astrologia, che l'ha rubato allo astrologo, e de filosofia, al filosofo, e che in effetto la poesia non ha propria sedia, ne la merita altramente, che d'un merchaio ragunatore di mercantie fatte da diversi artigiani.

ma la deità della scientia della pittura considera l'opere, cosi humane, come divine, le quali sono terminate dalle loro

less fatiguing, since you could stay in a cool place without moving about and exposing yourself to illness? But your soul could not enjoy the pleasures that come to it through the eyes, the windows of its habitation, it could not receive the reflections of bright places, it could not see the shady valleys watered by the play of meandering rivers, it could not see the many flowers which with their various colours compose harmonies for the eye, nor all the other things which may present themselves to the eye.

But if a painter on a cold and severe winter's day shows you his paintings of these or other country-sides where you once enjoyed yourself, beside some fountain, and where you can see yourself again in flowery meadows as a lover by the side of your beloved under the cool, soft shadows of green trees, will it not give you much greater pleasure than listening to the poet's description of such a scene?

Here the poet replies and concedes the above reasons, but says he is superior to the painter because he can make men talk and argue as he pleases, inventing things that do not exist; and that he will rouse men to take up arms, that he will describe the sky, the stars, and nature and the arts and all things. To which we reply that none of the things which he enumerates pertain to his own profession and that he must admit that in the making of speeches and orations he will be beaten by the orator; that in speaking of the stars he is stealing his subject from the astronomer, in speaking of philosophy, from the philosopher; and that as a matter of fact poetry has no domain of its own and does not deserve to have one any more than a monger who collects all sorts of goods from different makers.

But the deity of the science of painting extends over works human as well as divine in so far as they are bound by

superfitie, cioè linee de' termini de' corpi, con le quali ella comanda allo scultore la perfettione delle sue statue. questa col suo principio, cioè il disegno, insegna allo architettore fare, chel suo edifitio si renda grato al' occhio, questa alli componitori di diversi vasi, questa alli orefici, tessitori, recamatori; questa ha trovato li carratteri, con li quali si esprime li diuersi linguaggi, questa ha datto le caratte alli aritmetici, questa ha insegnato la figuratione alla geometria, questa insegna alli prospettivi et astrologi et alli machinatori e ingegneri.

surfaces, namely, the outlines of figures. With these she prescribes to the sculptor the perfection of his statues. By drawing, which is her beginning, she teaches the architect to make his edifices agreeable to the eye, she guides the potters in the making of various vases, the goldsmiths, the weavers and embroiderers. She has invented the characters in which the different languages are written, she has given the ciphers to the mathematician, and has described the figures of geometry, she teaches opticians, astronomers, mechanics, and engineers.[1]

Trat. 25]   28

DISPUTA DEL POETA E PITTORE, E CHE DIFERENTIA È DA POESIA A PITTURA

Dice il poeta, che la sua scientia è invenzione e misura; e questo è il semplice corpo di poesia, invenzione di materia e misura ne versi; e che lei si veste poi di tutte le scientie, al quale risponde il pittore, l'avere li medesimi obblighi nella scientia della pittura, cioè inventione e misura; inventione nella materia, che lui debbe fingere, e misura nelle cose dipinte, aciò non sieno sproportionate; ma che lui non si ueste tali tre scientie, anzi, che l'altre in gran parte si uestono della pittura, come l'astrologia, che nulla fa senza la prospettiua, la quale è principal membro d'essa pittura,—cioè l'astrologia matematica, non dico della fallace giudiciale, perdonemi, chi per mezzo delli

DISCUSSION BETWEEN THE POET AND THE PAINTER, AND WHAT IS THE DIFFERENCE BETWEEN POETRY AND PAINTING

The poet says that his science consists of invention and measure; invention as regards subject and measure as regards verse. This is the essence of poetry, its body, so to speak, which she then dresses up with all the sciences. The painter answers that similar principles govern the science of painting—invention and measure; invention as regards the subject-matter which he has to represent, and measure in the objects which he paints so that they should not be disproportioned; but that painting does not don the garments of the other three sciences, on the contrary, these partly clothe themselves in the garments of painting, as astrology[2] cannot do anything without perspective which is a principal part of painting. I am speaking of mathematical astrology and not of that fallacious divination by the stars. May those who make their living thereby from fools forgive me for saying so.

[1] Compare Leon Battista Alberti, *Della Pittura*, ii: 'Non si ritroverà arte alcuna, benchè abiettissima, che non abbi riguardo alla Pittura', and Francesco d'Hollanda, *Dialogo*, ii, where Michelangelo pays similar tribute to the art of painting. See p. 16.

[2] The term astrology in Leonardo's time covered both astrology and astronomy. Leonardo had in his possession the 'Acerba', by the learned Cecco d'Ascoli, Professor of Astrology at Bologna, a contemporary of Dante.

sciochi ne uiue. Dice il poeta, che de-
scriue una cosa, che ne rapresenta un' altra
piena di belle sentenze. il pittore dice
havere in arbitrio di far il medesimo, e
in questa parte anch' egli è poeta. e se 'l
poeta dice di far accendere gli homini
ad amare, è cosa principale della spetie
di tutti l'animali, il pittore a potentia di
fare il medesimo, e tanto più, che lui
mette inanzi all' amante la propria effigie
della cosa amata, il quale spesso fa con
quella bacciandola e parlandole con
quella quello, che non farebbe con le
medesime bellezze, posteli inanzi dal
scrittore e tanto più supera gl'ingegni de
li homini, ad amare et innamorarsi di
pittura, che non rapresenta alcuna donna
uiua. e già interuenne à me fare una
pittura, che rapresentaua una cosa diuina,
la quale comperata dall' amante di quella,
uolse leuarne la rapresentatione di tal
deità, per poterla baciare sanza sospetto.
ma infine la coscientia uinse li sospiri e
libidine, e fu forza, ch'ei se la leuasse di
casa. Hor ua tu, poeta, descriui una
bellezza sanza rapresentatione di cosa
uiua e desta li homini con quella a tali
desiderij. Se tu dirai: io ti descriuero
l'inferno, o 'l paradiso od altre delizie, o
spauenti, il pittore ti supera, perche ti
mettera inanzi cose, che tacendo diranno
tali delizie, o' ti spauenteranno e ti
moueranno l'animo à fugire. moue più
presto i sensi la pittura, che la poesia. e
se tu dirai che co'le parole tu leuerai un
popolo in pianto, o' in riso, io ti dirò,
che non sei tu, che muoue, egli è l'oratore, et una scientia, che non è poesia.
ma il pittore mouerà a riso, ma non à

The poet says that he can describe in
beautiful verse a thing which really
stands for something else by way of
simile. The painter replies that he can do
the same and that in this respect he too
is a poet. And if the poet says that he can
kindle love[1] in men which is the main
motive of the species in the whole animal
world, the painter has the power to do
the same, the more so as he can place the
true image of the beloved before the
lover, who often kisses it and speaks to
it, a thing he would not do to the description of the same beauties by the writer.
The painter's power over men's minds
is even greater, for he can induce them to
love and fall in love with a picture which
does not portray any living woman. It
once happened to me that I made a picture representing a sacred subject which
was bought by one who loved it and
who then wished to remove the symbols
of divinity in order that he might kiss
her without misgivings. Finally his
conscience prevailed over his sighs and
lust and he felt constrained to remove
the picture from his house. Now let the
poet go and try to rouse such desires in
men by the description of a beauty
which does not portray any living being.
And if you say: I shall describe hell for
you, and paradise[2] or any other delights
or terrors, there too the painter is your
superior because he will place things
before you which though silent will
express such delights or terrors that will
turn your courage into flight.

Painting will move the senses more
readily than poetry. And if you say that
with words you will move a people to
tears or to laughter, my reply is that it is
not the poet who moves, but the orator,
by another science than poetry. But the
painter will move you to laughter[3] and
not to tears, because weeping implies a

[1] For the power of poetry to kindle passions
compare Plato, *Rep.* x. 660; Aristotle, *Poet.* vi.
2, and *Pol.* viii. 7.

[2] As Dante in his *Divina Commedia*.
[3] Compare p. 38.

K

pianto, perch' el pianto è maggior accidente, che non è 'l riso.

Uno pittore fece una figura, che, chi
la uedeua subito sbadigliaua, e tanto
replicaua tale accidente, quanto si teneua
gli occhi alla pittura, la quale anchora lei
era finta sbadigliare. Altri hanno dipinto
atti libidinosi e tanto lussuriosi, che
hanno incitati li risguardatori di quella
alla medesima festa, il che non farà la
poesia.

E se tu scriuerai la figura d'alcuni dei,
non sarà tale scrittura nella medesima
ueneratione, che la iddea dipinta, perchè
a tale pittura sarà fatto di continuo uoti
et diuerse orazioni, et a quella concorre-
rano uarie generationi di diuerse pro-
uincie e per li mari orientali, e da tali si
dimanderà soccorso a tal pittura, e non
alla scrittura.

more violent agitation than laughter.
An artist painted a picture that whoever
saw it at once yawned, and went on
doing so as long as he kept his eyes on the
picture, which represented a person who
also was yawning. Other artists have
represented acts of wantonness and lust
which kindled these passions in the beholders. Poetry could not do as much.
And if you write a description of Gods,
such writing will never be worshipped
in the same way as a painting of the
deity.[1] For to the picture many offerings
and prayers will incessantly flow, many
generations will flock to it from distant
lands and from over the eastern Seas,
and they will ask for help from such a
painting, but not from writing.[2]

Trat. 26]   29

ARGUITIONE DEL POETA CONTRA 'L PITTORE

Tu dici, o pittore, chella tua arte è
adorata, ma non imputare a te tal uirtù,
ma alla cosa, di che tal pittura è rapre-
sentatrice. qui il pittore risponde: o tu,
poeta, che ti fai anchora tu imitatore,
perchè non rappresenti tu co' le tue
parole cose, che le lettere tue, conteni-
trici d'esse parolle, anchora loro sieno
adorate? ma la natura ha più fauorito il

THE POET'S ARGUMENT AGAINST THE PAINTER

You say, oh painter, that your art is
the object of worship. Do not ascribe a
power to yourself which is due to the
subject of your painting. The painter
then replies: 'Oh poet, you who likewise
try to imitate us, why don't you choose
a subject for your poem that will move
people to worship the written letters of
your words in the same way?'

[1] Compare Leon Battista Alberti, *Della
Pittura*, ii: 'Che la Pittura ci abbi espresso gli
Dii, che sono reveriti dalle genti e da pensare
che ciò sia stato un grandissimo dono con-
cesso a'mortali. Conciossiachè la Pittura ha
giovato troppo grandemente alla religione,
mediante la quale noi siamo principalmente
congiunti agli Dii, ed al persevare gli animi
con una certa intera religione. Dicono che
Fidia fece in Elide un Giove la bellezza del
quale aggiunse assai alla già conceputa
religione.'
The statue of Zeus at Olympia was thus
described by one who saw it: 'When you
stand before it you forget every misfortune
of our earthly life so great is the splendour

and beauty of the artist's creation' (Dion
Chrysostomos, *Orat.* xii. 51).
[2] However, poetry has an advantage, as
Pindar pointed out, in not being fixed to one
place; and while people have to travel from
afar to see a picture or statue, poems can travel
to them. In a beautiful passage (*Nem.* v, *ad
init.*) the Greek poet recognizes sculpture and
poetry as sister arts and contrasts the merely
local influence of a statue commemorating an
athlete with the wide diffusion of the poem.
'No sculptor I, to fashion images that shall
stand idly on one pedestal for ever, no, go
forth from Aegina, sweet song of mine, on
every freighted ship, on each light bark.'

pittore ch'el poeta, e meritamente l'
opere del fauorito debbono essere più
onorate, che di quello, che non è in
fauore. Adonque laudiamo quello, che
con le parolle satisfa al audito, e quel che
con la pittura satisfa al contento del
uedere, ma tanto meno quel delle parole,
quanto elle sono accidentali e create da
minor autore, che l'opere di natura, di
che 'l pittore è imitatore, la qual natura
è terminante dentro alle figure delle lor
superfitie.

But nature has favoured the painter
more than the poet; and more honour is
due to the works of one favoured than
to the works of one not so favoured.

Let us therefore give praise both to
him who delights our ears with words
and to him who with painting delights
our sight; but less praise is due to him
who uses words, as they are but accidental designations created by man, who
is inferior to the creator of the works of
nature which the painter imitates.

And nature is enclosed within the surfaces of shapes.

Trat. 27]   30

RISPOSTA DEL RE MATTIA[1] AD UN POETA,
CHE GAREGGIAUA CON UN PITTORE

THE REPLY OF KING MATHIAS[1] TO A POET
WHO COMPETED WITH A PAINTER

Portando il di del nattale del Re Mattia
un poeta un' opera fattagli in laude del

On King Mathias' birthday a poet
brought him a poem composed in praise

[1] There are analogies between this scene
and the meeting of poet and painter in
Shakespeare's *Timon of Athens*, Act I. I. Here
too a noble patron decides in favour of painting. Mathias Corvinus, King of Hungary,
was a patron of the arts (Vasari, ed. Milanesi,
iii. 467). Lorenzo il Magnifico presented him
with two busts by Verrocchio and other works
(Vasari, iii. 361). Lodovico Sforza asked a
great painter, probably Leonardo, to paint a
picture of the Madonna for him. He says in
a letter to Maffeo da Treviglio, ambassador to
the King, dated April 13, 1485: '. . . et perche
havemo inteso che la sua maestà se delecta
multo de belle picture, presertim che habino
in se qualche devotione, ritrovandose de
presente qua uno optimo pictore, al quale,
havendo veduto experientia del ingenio suo,
non cognoscemo pare, havemo dato ordine
cum epso pictore, che ne faccia una figura de
Nostra Donna quanto bella excellente et
devota la sapia più fare, senza sparagno di
spesa alcuna, et se acinga ad l'opera de
presente, ne faccia altro lavoro finchè l'abia
finita, la quale poi manderemo ad donare a la
prefata Sua Maestà' (*Monumenta Hungaria
Historica*, Budapest, 1877, p. 41). Bernardino
Corio describes the King's voyage through
Pavia and Milan in March 1474, with an escort
of three hundred horsemen and travelling in

a coach covered by a cloth of gold and drawn
by four white horses. He calls him King of
Dacia, a man of grave demeanour with a long
white beard. The Sforzas gave him a magnificent reception. On being shown the treasure
in the castle of Pavia he expressed the opinion
that it was not becoming to a prince to amass
wealth. The library of Pavia was more to his
liking, since he was himself the owner of a
famous library at Budapest and a bibliophile
(Vasari, iii. 239). The cordial relations with
the Sforzas led to an engagement in 1487
between John Corvinus, the king's natural
son and destined heir, and Bianca Maria, the
sister of Duke Gian Galeazzo. For this occasion Bellincioni composed a sonnet on the
beauty of the bride:

'Biancha di perle, bella piu ch'el sole
Dell' ingegno del padre in se raccolse,
E la bellezza da la madre tolse,
Che 'l volto ha di rubin rose e viole.'

The engagement was broken off after the
death of the King in 1490, his son having
failed to secure the throne; and Bianca Maria
was married to the Emperor Maximilian. It
may be that Leonardo's story of King Mathias
pronouncing judgement on the comparative
merits of a sonnet and a portrait is founded on
an actual occurrence.

giorno, ch'esso re era (nato) a beneficio del mondo, et un pittore gli presentò un ritratto della sua innamorata, subito il re rinchiuse il libro del poeta, e uoltossi alla pittura, et à quella fermò la uista con grande ammiratione. allora il poeta forte isdegnato disse: O Re, leggi, leggi, e sentirai cosa di maggiore sustantia, che una mutta pittura. Allora il re, sentendosi riprender del risguardare cose mutte, disse: o poeta, taci tu, che non sai ciò, che ti dica; questa pittura serue a miglior senso, che la tua, la quale è da orbi. dammi cosa, ch'io la possa uedere e toccare, et non che solamente la possa udire, e non biasmare la mia ellettione del' hauermi io messa la tua opera sotto 'l gomito e questa del pittore tengo con due le mani, dandola alli miei occhi; perchè le mani da lor medesime hanno tolte a seruire a più degno senso, che non è l'udire. et io per me giudico, che tale proportione sia dalla scientia del pittore à quella del poeta, qual' è dalli suoi sensi, de' quali questi si fanno obietti. non sai tu, che la nostra anima è composta d' armonia, et armonia non s'ingenera, se non in istanti, ne quali le proportionalità delli obietti si fan uedere, o' udire? Non uedi, che nella tua scientia non è proportionalità creata in istante, anzi, l'una parte nasce dall' altra successiuamente, e non nasce la succedente, se l'antecedente non more? Per questo giudico la tua inuentione esser assai inferiore à quella del pittore, solo perchè da quello non componesi proportionalità armonica. Essa non contenta la mente del' auditore, o' ueditore, come fa la proportionalità delle bellissime membra, componitrici delle diuine bellezze di questo uiso, che m'è dinanzi, le quali, in un medesimo tempo tutte insieme gionte, mi danno tanto piacere con la loro diuina proportione, che null'

[1] Plato, *Timaeus*, 47; Aristotle, *De Anima*, A. 4, 408.

of the event which he said was for the benefit of the world, and a painter presented him with a portrait of his beloved. The King quickly closed the book of the poet and turning to the picture fixed his eyes on it with great admiration. Then the poet very indignantly said: 'Oh King, read, but read, and you will learn matter of far weightier substance than a mute picture.' Then the King, resenting the reproach that he was admiring mute things, said: 'Silence, oh poet, you do not know what you are saying; this picture serves a nobler sense than your work which might be for the blind. Give me something that I can see and touch and not only hear, and do not blame my choice when I put your book under my arm and am holding the painting with both hands for my eyes to enjoy; because my hands chose of their own accord to serve the nobler sense and not the sense of hearing. I myself am of the opinion that the painter's science is as far above the poet's as the sense which he serves is nobler. Do you not know that our soul is composed of harmony[1] and that harmony is only produced when proportions of things are seen or heard simultaneously? And do you not see that in your science there is no simultaneous reaction of proportions, but one part engenders another in succession so that the latter is not born before the former has died? Therefore, in my opinion, your invention is much inferior to the painter's for the sole reason that there is no composition of harmonious proportions.[2] It does not satisfy the mind of the listener or beholder like the proportions of the beautiful forms that compose the divine beauties of this face here before me, which being all joined together and reacting simultaneously give me so much pleasure with their divine proportion that I think there is no

[2] Compare Lessing, *Laokoon*, xvii, xx–xxii, and p. 49.

altra cosa giudico essere sopra la terra fatta dal homo, che dar la possa maggiore.

Non è si insensato giuditio, che, s'eglie preposto, qual è più da elleggere, o' stare in perpetue tenebre, o' uoler perdere l'audito, che subito non dica uolere più tosto perdere l'udito insieme con l'odorato, prima che restar ciecho. perchè, chi perde il uedere, perde la bellezza del mondo con tutte le forme delle cose create, e il sordo sol perde il suono fatto dal moto del' aria percossa, ch'è minima cosa nel mondo.

Tu, che dici la scientia esser tanto più nobile, quanto essa s'estende in più degno subietto, e per questo più uale una falsa immaginatione della essentia d'iddio, che una immaginatione d'una cosa men degna, e per questo diremo, la pittura, la qual sol s'estende nell' opere d'iddio esser più degna chella poesia che solo s'estende in buggiadre fintioni de l'opere humane. con debita lamentatione si dole la pittura per esser lei scacciata del numero delle arti liberali, conciosiachè essa sia uera figliuola della natura et operata da più degno senso. Onde attorto, o scrittori, l'hauete lasciata fori del numero delle dett' arti liberali; conciosiachè questa, non ch'alle opere di natura, ma ad infinite attende, che la natura mai le creò.

other work of man on earth that can give greater pleasure.

There is nobody so senseless who when given the choice of either remaining in perpetual darkness or losing his hearing will not at once say that he prefers to lose his hearing and his sense of smell as well rather than be blind. Because whoever loses his eyesight loses the beauty of the world with all the forms in creation, whereas deafness only brings the loss of sound, caused by motion arising from the percussion of the air, which is a very small matter.

To you, who maintain that the nobility of a science depends on the worthiness of the object which it pursues and say that some mistaken conception about the essence of God is worth more than the representation of something less lofty, we shall reply that painting extending as it does to the works of God is nobler than poetry which only deals with fabricated stories about the deeds of men.

Painting has every right to complain of being driven out from the number of Liberal Arts, since she is a true daughter of nature and employs the noblest of all the senses. It was wrong, oh writers, to leave her out from the number of Liberal Arts, because she deals not only with the works of nature but extends over an infinite number of things which nature never created.

CONCLUSIONE INFRA 'L POETA ET IL PITTORE

Poi che noi habbiamo concluso, la poesia esser in sommo grado di comprensione alli ciechi, et che la pittura fa il medesimo alli sordi, noi diremo: tanto di più ualere la pittura, che la poesia, quanto la pittura serue à miglior senso

CONCLUSION OF THE DISCUSSION BETWEEN POET AND PAINTER

Having come to the conclusion that poetry is for the blind the supreme degree of understanding and that painting is the same for the deaf, we may say that the value of painting is greater than that of poetry in so far as it serves a better and nobler sense.

et più nobile, che la poesia; la qual nobiltà è prouata essere tripla alla nobilità di tre altri sensi, perchè è stato elletto di uolere più presto perdere l'audito et odorato e tatto, ch'el senso del uedere. perchè, chi perde il uedere, perde la ueduta e bellezza de l'uniuerso e resta a similitudine d'un che sia chiuso in uita in una sepoltura, nella quale habbia moto e uita. Hor non uedi tu, che l'occhio abbraccia la bellezza di tutt' il mondo? egli è capo dell' astrologia; egli fa la cosmografia, esso tutte le humane arti consiglia e coregge, moue l'homo à diuerse parti del mondo; questo è principe delle matematiche, le sue scientie sono certissime; questo ha misurato l'altezze e grandezze delle stelle, questo ha trovato gli elementi e loro siti. questo ha fatto predire le cose future mediante il corso delle stelle, questo l'architettura, e prospettiva, questo la diuina pittura a generata. O, eccellentissimo sopra tutte l'altre cose create da dio! quali laudi fien quelle, ch'esprimere possino la tua nobiltà? quali populi, quale lingue saranno quelle, che possino a' pieno descriuere la tua uera operatione? Questo è finestra del' human corpo, per la quale la sua via specula e fruisce la bellezza del mondo, per questo l'anima si contenta dello humano carcere, e sanza questo esso humano carcere è suo tormento. per questo la industria humana ha trouato il fuocho, mediante il quale l'occhio riacquista quello, che prima li tolsero le tenebre. Questo a ornato la natura con l'agricoltura e diletteuoli giardini. Ma che bisogna, ch'io m'estenda in si alto e lungho discorso, quale è quella cosa, che per lui non si faccia? ei moue li huomini

The nobility of the sense of sight was shown to be three times greater than that of the other three senses, since it was thought preferable to lose the senses of hearing, smell, and touch rather than the sense of sight, because whoso loses his eyesight is deprived of vision and of the beauty of the universe and may be likened to one buried alive in a grave where he can move and subsist. Now do you not see that the eye embraces the beauty of the whole world? It is the lord of astronomy and the maker of cosmography; it counsels and corrects all the arts of mankind; it leads men to the different parts of the world; it is the prince of mathematics, and the sciences founded on it are absolutely certain. It has measured the distances and sizes of the stars; it has found the elements and their locations; it divines the future from the course of the stars; it has given birth to architecture, and to perspective, and to the divine art of painting.

Oh excellent thing, superior to all others created by God! What praises can do justice to your nobility? What peoples, what tongues will fully describe your true function? The eye is the window of the human body through which it feels its way and enjoys the beauty of the world. Owing to the eye the soul is content to stay in its bodily prison, for without it such bodily prison is torture.

With the help of the eye human industry discovered fire, by means of which the eye regains that whereof darkness had formerly deprived it. The eye decorated nature with agriculture and delightful gardens.

But what need is there for me to expand this subject with exalted and long discourse—what is there that can be done without the eye? It moves men from

dal oriente all' occidente, questo ha trouato la nauigatione; et in questo supera la natura, perche li semplici naturali sono finiti, e l'opere, che l'occhio commanda alle mani, sono infinite, come dimostra 'l pittore nelle fintioni d'infinite forme d'animali ed herbe, e piante et siti.

Fine in quanto di poesia e pittura.

east to west. It has invented navigation and it is superior to nature in that simple natural objects are finite, but the works which our hands perform at the command of the eye are infinite, as is shown by the painters' invention of infinite forms of animals and herbs—of plants and scenes.[1]

End as regards poetry and painting.

[1] Francisco Goya in his announcement of the *Caprichos* in 1799 said: 'Painting, like poetry, selects in the universe whatever she deems most appropriate to her ends. She assembles in a single fantastic personage circumstances and features which nature distributes among many individuals. From this combination ingeniously composed, results the happy imitation by virtue of which the artist earns the title of inventor and not of servile copyist.'

III

PAINTING, POETRY, AND MUSIC

'That longing for harmony in which all senses combine.'—LEONARDO.

IN comparing Painting and Poetry there is a tendency to review their representational and didactic aspects. But if we turn to Music in our comparison, these aspects are more inaccessible to observation, being subordinated to the more direct appeal of sound alone. Here the power of reducing multitude to unity of effect is revealed more clearly; and we naturally revert to considerations of form, and to the mathematical foundations of the arts.

Harmony of proportions is inherent in different ways in the visual arts, where it is produced by the relation of the parts to the whole, and in the art of Music, where sounds of different pitch played simultaneously blend into one chord.

Leon Battista Alberti identified architectural proportions with the numerical proportions of musical intervals. 'The same numbers which by their relation in the harmony of voices sound pleasing to the ears of man also fill his eyes and soul with rare pleasure.' As author of the theory he designates the Greek philosopher Pythagoras, who is said to have discovered the dependence of musical intervals on numerical proportions (*De re Aedificatoria*, ix. 5).[1]

Leonardo was alive to these correspondences. He felt that proportions were like a musical chord sounded all at one time (pp. 68, 72, Trat. 29, 32) and these simultaneous harmonies gave him intense delight. 'There is no other work of man on earth that can give greater pleasure' (p. 63, Trat. 27).[2]

Poetry cannot awaken this sublime harmony in our spirit since she can only utter one word at a time.[3] But, though she is unable to reproduce Music's perpendicular chord, she can imitate the horizontal line of her melody and her rhythmical movement. The syllables of her words

---

[1] Leonardo established a law whereby the same numerical proportions apply to musical intervals and to the sizes of objects receding into space. (Trat. 31, p. 69, and R. 102.)

[2] 'And I know not if save in this, such gift be allowed to man,

That out of three sounds he frame, not a fourth sound but a star.'
(Browning, *Abt Vogler.*)

[3] 'Hearing excites the mind by slow degrees The man is warmed at once by what he sees.' (Horace, *Ars Poetica.*)

are the equivalent in verse of the musician's notes. Both verse and voice proceed through time in rhythmical formation.

Painting, on the other hand, though unable to represent these invisible and temporal metres and rhythms that reach the ear, may evoke a similar emotion by drawing lines through space.

'The line may be likened to the length of a certain period of time; and just as a line begins and terminates in a point, so such a period of time begins and terminates in an instant. And, whereas a line is infinitely divisible, the divisibility of a period of time is of the same nature; and as the divisions of the line may bear a certain proportion to each other, so may the divisions of time' (R. 916).

Hence the flowing outlines in the visual arts may be considered the equivalents in space of the poet's and musician's rhythmic movements in time (p. 74, Trat. 29).

Before Leonardo, Plutarch had compared contours to movement in dancing: 'Dancing resembles the lines by which figures are defined', and he proceeded: 'Dancing is like silent poetry, while Poetry is the dance of speech' (*Quaestiones Conviviales*, 748 A, B). But Painting excels because she is able to transmit similar rhythmical effects all at once and independent of time (pp. 74, 75, Trat. 29, 30; R. 1131 A).

It follows from these considerations that harmony and rhythm pass beyond the limits of one art. They are inherent in painting, sculpture, and architecture, in poetry and music, and we might add in dancing also. They respond to a feeling for beauty in our very being, and reveal themselves in different attire according to the conditions of each art.[1] 'Harmony has motions akin to the revolutions in our own souls' said Plato (*Timaeus*, 47), and Leonardo re-echoed: 'Do you not know that our soul is composed of harmony?' (p. 68, Trat. 27).

[1] It will be of interest to compare the views of some recent writers on the formal correspondences in music and the other arts. According to Walter Pater all art constantly aspires towards music: 'That the mere matter of a poem, for instance its subject, namely its given incidents or situation, that the mere matter of a picture, the actual circumstances of an event, the topography of a landscape, should be nothing without the form, the spirit of the handling, that this form, this mode of handling, should become an end in itself, should penetrate every part of the matter, this is what all art constantly strives after and achieves in different degrees' (*Essay on School of Giorgione, Renaissance*).

And Edgar Allan Poe asserted that the musical element of sound is of great importance, while truth of faithfulness to fact is of small importance to the poet.

Paul Valéry described certain modern poets who, while keeping to the traditional forms of French verse, set themselves to eliminate descriptions, precepts, moralities, and arbitrary precisions. 'They purged their poetry of almost every intellectual element that cannot

L

Trat. 29]   32

COME LA MUSICA SI DE' CHIAMARE SORELLA ET MINORE DELLA PITTURA	MUSIC MAY JUSTLY BE CALLED THE YOUNGER SISTER OF PAINTING

La Musica non è da essere chiamata altro, che sorella della pittura, conciosiach' essa è subietto dell' audito, secondo senso al occhio, e compone armonia con le congiontioni delle sue parti proportionali operate nel medesimo tempo, costrette à nascere e morire in uno o più tempi armonici, li quali tempi circondano la proportionalità de' membri, di che tale armonia si compone non altrimenti, che si faccia la linea circonferentiale le membra, di che si genera la bellezza umana. ma la pittura eccelle e signoreggia la musica, perch' essa non more imediate dopo la sua creatione, come fa la sventurata musica,[1] anzi resta in essere e ti si dimostra in vita quel, che in fatto è una sola superfitie. o maravigliosa scientia, tu riservi in vita le caduche bellezze de' mortali, le quali hanno più permanentia, che l'opere di natura, le quali al continuo sono uariate dal tempo, chelle conduce alla debita uecchiezza. e tale scientia ha tale proportione con la divina natura, quale hanno le sue opere con le opere d'essa natura, e per questo è adorata.

Music cannot be called otherwise than the sister of painting, for she is dependent upon hearing, a sense second to sight, and her harmony is composed of the union of its proportional parts sounded simultaneously, rising and falling in one or more harmonic rhythms. These rhythms may be said to surround the proportionality of the members composing the harmony, just as the contour bounds the members from which human beauty is born.

But painting excels and ranks higher than music, because it does not fade away as soon as it is born, as is the fate of unhappy music.[1] On the contrary, it endures and has all the appearance of being alive, though in fact it is confined to one surface. Oh wonderful science, which can preserve the transient beauty of mortals and endow it with a permanence greater than the works of nature; for these are subject to the continual changes of time which leads them towards inevitable old age! And such a science is in the same relation to divine nature as its works are to the works of nature, and for this it is to be adored.

be expressed in music' (*Variétés*). Stéphane Mallarmé's aim was 'achever la transposition, au livre, de la symphonie'.

'Painting, which may be defined as a disposition of colours on a plane surface, appeals to our senses directly, without the intervention of images or logical concepts, in the same way that music does' (Herbert Read). 'As music is the poetry of sound, so painting is the poetry of sight and the subject-matter has nothing to do with harmony of sound or of colour.' J. McN. Whistler.

'Braque paints nature as one plays music. His conception of space in painting is like silence in music' (Stanislas Fumet).

[1] Leonardo made a point of proving that painting was as lasting as sculpture (pp. 100, 97, Trat. 38, 37) and more lasting than music because he wished to prove that painting was an equal of the sciences which ranked with the Liberal Arts; and durability or rather invariability was in scholastic circles thought to be a necessary attribute of all science. Compare Aristotle, *Nicomachean Ethics*, vi. 3: 'We all suppose that what we know with scientific knowledge is invariable; but of that which is variable we cannot say so soon as it is out of sight whether it is in existence or not. The object of science then is necessary. Therefore it is eternal: for whatever is of its own nature necessary is eternal: and what is eternal neither begins nor ceases to be.'

Trat. 30]   33

PARLA IL MUSICO COL PITTORE

Dice il musico, che la sua scientia è da essere equiparata a quella del pittore, perchè essa compone un corpo di molte membra, del quale lo speculatore contempla tutta la sua gratia in tanti tempi armonici, quanti sono li tempi, nelli quali essa nasce e muore, e con quelli tempi trastulla con gratia l'anima, che risiede nel corpo del suo contemplante. ma il pittore risponde e dice, che il corpo composto delle humane membra non da di se piacere a' tempi armonici, nelli quali essa bellezza abbia a variarsi, dando figuratione ad un altro, ne che in essi tempi abbia a nascere e morire, ma lo fa permanente per moltissimi anni, et è di tanta eccellentia, che la riserva in vita quella armonia delle proportionate membra, le quali natura con tutte sue forze conservare non potrebbe. quante pitture hanno conservato il simulacro d'una divina bellezza, ch'el tempo o' morte in breve ha distrutto il suo naturale esempio, et è restata più degna l'opera del pittore, che della natura sua maestra!

THE MUSICIAN SPEAKS TO THE PAINTER

The musician claims that his science is equal to that of the painter, for it, too, is a body composed of many parts—the graces of which may be contemplated by the observer in as many harmonic rhythms as there are, and with these rhythms which are born and die it delights the soul of man within him. But the painter answers and says that the human body composed of many members does not give pleasure in harmonic rhythms in which beauty has to vary and create new forms, nor is it composed in rhythms which constantly require to be born and to die, but he makes it to last a great number of years, and of such excellence that it keeps alive that harmony of proportion which Nature with all its force could not keep. How many paintings have preserved the image of divine beauty of which time or sudden death have destroyed Nature's original, so that the work of the painter has survived in nobler form than that of Nature, his mistress.[1]

Trat. 31]   34

IL PITTORE DÀ I GRADI DELLE COSE OPPOSTE ALL' OCCHIO, COME 'L MUSICO DÀ DELLE VOCI OPPOSTE ALL' ORECCHIO

THE PAINTER MEASURES THE DISTANCE OF THINGS AS THEY RECEDE FROM THE EYE BY DEGREES JUST AS THE MUSICIAN MEASURES THE INTERVALS OF THE VOICES HEARD BY THE EAR

Benchè le cose opposte all' occhio si tocchino l'un e l'altra di mano in mano,

Although objects observed by the eye touch one another as they recede, I shall

[1] Sonnet by Bernardo Bellincioni on a portrait by Leonardo of Cecilia Gallerani, mistress of Lodovico il Moro.

Sopra il retracto di Madona Cicilia qual fece maestro Leonardo.

Poeta—Di che te adiri? a chi invidia hai natura?

Natura—Al Vinci, che ha ritrato una tua stella;
Cecilia, si bellissima hoggi è quella
Che a' suoi begli occhi el sol par umbra oscura.

Poeta—L'honor è tuo, se ben con tua pictura
La fa che par che ascolti e non favella.

Pensa, quanto sarà più viva e bella
Più a te fia gloria in ogni età futura.
Ringratiar dunque Ludovico or poi
Et l'ingegno e la man di Leonardo
Che a' posteri di lei voglian far parte.
Chi lei vedrà cosi, benchè sia tardo
Vederla viva, dirà: basti ad noi
Comprender or quel che è natura et arte.

Leonardo's portrait of Lucrezia Crivelli inspired the Latin verses written by an unknown Latin poet on a sheet in the Codice Atlantico (R. 1560).

nondimeno farò la mia regola di XX. in. XX. braccia, come ha fatto il musico infra le voci, che benchè la sia unita et appiccha insieme, nondimeno a pochi gradi di voce in voce, domandando quella prima, seconda, terza, quarta e quinta, et così di grado in grado ha posto nomi alla varietà d'alzare et bassare la voce.

Se tu o musico dirai, che la pittura è meccanica per essere operata con l'esercitio delle mani, e la musica è operata con la bocca, ch'è organo humano, ma non pel conto del senso del gusto, come la mano senso del tatto. meno degne sono anchora le parolle ch'e' fatti; ma tu scrittore delle scientie, non copij tu con mano, scrivendo ciò, che sta nella mente, come fa il pittore? e se tu dicessi la musica essere composta di proporzione, o io con questa medesima seguito la pittura, come mi vedrai.

nevertheless found my rule on a series of intervals measuring 20 braccia each, just as the musician who, though his voices are united and strung together, has created intervals according to the distance from voice to voice, calling them unison, second, third, fourth, and fifth, and so on, until names have been given to the various degrees of pitch proper to the human voice.[1]

If you, oh musician, say that painting is a mechanical art because it is performed with the use of hands, you must admit that music is performed with the mouth which is also a human organ. And the mouth is not working in this case for the sense of taste, just as the hands while painting are not working for the sense of touch!

Words are of less account than performances.[2] But you, oh writer on the sciences, do you not, like the painter, copy by hand that which is in the mind?

If you say that Music is composed of proportion, then I have used similar means in Painting, as I shall show.

Trat. 31*b*]

34*a*

Quella cosa è più degna, che satisfa a miglior senso. adonque la pittura, satisfatrice al senso del vedere, è più nobile che la musica, che solo satisfa all' udito.

Quella cosa è più nobile, che ha più eternità. Adonque la musica, che si va consumando mentre ch'ella nasce, è men

That thing is most worthy which satisfies the highest sense. Therefore as Painting satisfies the sense of seeing she is more noble than Music which only satisfies the ear.

That thing is noblest which has the longest duration. Therefore Music, which passes away as soon as it is born,

[1] 'Farò la mia regola di XX in XX braccia.' This is a reference to Leonardo's theory (see R. 99–106) that objects of equal size placed so as to recede at regular intervals of, say, 20 braccia, each diminish to one-half, one-third, one-quarter of their size, and so on, in harmonic progression. There is therefore a close analogy with the division of the string on the monochord producing the octave, fifth, and fourth, &c.

Leon Battista Alberti distrusted the application of the proportions to perspective ('Klei-

nere kunsttheor. Schr. von H. Janitschek', *Wiener Quellensch.* ix, p. 81) and Euclid, *Optico.*, Theorem 8, says: 'The appearance of equal and parallel magnitudes, when placed at unequal intervals from the eye, is not in proportion to the distances.' It was left to Leonardo to explore this field.

[2] Compare Pomponius Gauricus (*De Sculptura*, edition 1886, p. 100): 'Scriptores quidem agunt verbis, at vero Sculptores rebus: Illi narrant, Hi vero exprimunt explicant'.

degna che la pittura, che con uetri si fa eterna.

Quella cosa, che contiene in se più universalità e varietà di cose, quella fia detta di più eccellentia. adonque la pittura è da essere preposta a tutte le operationi, perchè è contenitrice di tutte le forme, che sono, e di quelle, che non sono in natura; è più da essere magnificata et esaltata, che la musica, che solo attende alla voce.

Con questa si fa i simulacri alli dij, dintorno a questa si fa il culto divino, il quale è ornato con la musica a questa seruente; con questa si dà copia alli amanti della causa de' loro amori, con questa si riserua le bellezze, le quali il tempo e la natura fa fugitive, con questa noi riserviamo le similitudini degli huomini famosi, e se tu dicessi la musica s'eterna con lo scriverla, el medesimo facciamo noi qui cō le lettere. Adonque, poi chè tu hai messo la musica infra le arti liberali, o tu vi metti questa, o tu ne levi quella, e se tu dicessi li huomini vili la d'operano, e così è guasta la musica da chi non la sa.

is of less account than Painting which, protected by glaze, lasts for ever. That which contains within itself the greatest number of qualities and varieties may be said to be the most excellent.

Therefore Painting is to be preferred to all other operations because it can produce all the forms which are and which are not in nature, it is more to be praised and exalted than Music which is concerned with the voice alone.

With Painting the images of Gods are made; round Painting are held divine rites which the Music serves to adorn. Lovers come to it for portraits of those they love, and by its means beauty is preserved which otherwise Nature and Time would destroy; by it we preserve the likenesses of our famous men. And if you should say that Music also lasts for ever if written down, we are doing the same here with letters.

After giving a place to Music among the Liberal Arts you must place Painting there, too, or else withdraw Music.

And if you say that there are vile painters, I reply that Music also can be spoiled by those who do not understand it.

Trat. 31c]

34b

Se tu dirai le scientie non mecaniche sono le mentali, io ti dirò che la pittura è mentale, e ch'ella, sicome la musica e geometria considera le proportioni delle quantità continue, e l'aritmetica delle discontinue, questa considera tutte le quantità continue e le qualità delle proportioni d'ombre e lumi e distantie nella sua prospettiva.

If you say that the Sciences are not 'mechanical' but purely of the mind, I reply that Painting is of the mind and that just as Music and Geometry deal with the proportions of continuous quantities and Arithmetic with non-continuous quantities, Painting deals with all continuous quantities, and it deals besides with the qualities of proportions, shadows and light and distances in perspective.

Trat. 31a]

34c

Dopo questa (la pittura) viene la scultura, arte dignissima, ma non di tanta eccellentia d'ingegno operata, concio-

After Painting comes Sculpture, a very noble art, but one that does not in the execution require the same supreme ingenuity as the art of painting, since in

siachè in due casi principali sia dificilis-
sima, co' quali il pittore procede nella
sua, questa è aiutata dalla natura, cioè
prospettiva, ombra e lumi. questa anchora non è imitatrice de' colori, per li
quali il pittore si affatica a trovare, che le
ombre sieno compagne de' lumi.

two most important and difficult particulars, in foreshortening and in light
and shade, for which the painter has to
invent a process, sculpture is helped by
nature. Moreover, Sculpture does not
imitate colour which the painter takes
pains to attune so that the shadows accompany the lights.

Trat. 32]   35

CONCLUSIONE DEL POETA, PITTORE E MUSICO

CONCLUSION OF THE DISCUSSION BETWEEN THE POET, THE PAINTER, AND THE MUSICIAN

Tal diferentia è inquanto alla figuratione delle cose corporee dal pittore e
poeta, quanto dalli corpi smembrati a li
uniti, perchè il poeta nel descrivere la
bellezza o' brutezza di qualonche corpo
te lo dimostra a membro a membro et in
diversi tempi, et il pittore tel fa vedere
tutto in un tempo. el poeta non può
porre con le parole la vera figura delle
membra di che si compone un tutto, com
el pittore, il quale tel pone innanti con
quella verità, ch'è possibile in natura; et
al poeta accade il medesimo, come al
musico, che canta sol' un canto composto
di quattro cantori, e canta prima il canto,
poi il tenore, e cosi seguita il contr' alto e
poi il basso; e di costui non risulta la
gratia della proportionalità armonica, la
quale si rinchiude in tempi armonici, e
fa esso poeta a similitudine d'un bel
volto, il quale ti si mostra a membro a
membro, che cosi facendo, non rimar-
resti mai satisfatto dalla sua bellezza, la
quale solo consiste nella divina proportionalità delle predette membra insieme
composte, le quali solo in un tempo
compongono essa divina armonia d'esso
congionto di membre, che spesso tol-
gono la libertà posseduta a chi le vede.
e la musica ancora fa nel suo tempo

There is the same difference between
the poet's and the painter's representa-
tions of the human figure as there is
between dismembered bodies and un-
divided bodies. Because the poet in describing the beauty or ugliness of any
figure can only show it to you consecu-
tively, bit by bit, while the painter will
display it all at once.[1] The poet is unable
with words to show you the true images of the parts which make up the
whole, while the painter will display
them for you as truthfully as only nature
can do. And the poet's way may be
compared to that of a musician who all
by himself undertakes to sing a composition which is intended for four voices
and first sings the part of the soprano,
then that of the tenor, then the contralto,
and finally the bass. Such performances
cannot produce the beauty of harmonious proportions set in harmonious
divisions of time.

Again, the poet's work may be likened
to a beautiful face which is shown to you
feature by feature so that you can never
appreciate its beauty, which rests en-
tirely on the divine proportions relating
the parts to one another. The features
must react together and simultaneously
in order to produce that divine harmony
which often so captivates the spectator
that he loses his liberty.

[1] See p. 49.

armonico le soavi melodie composte delle sue varie voci, delle quali il poeta è privato della loro discretione armonica, e ben che la poesia entri pel senso dell' audito alla sedia del giuditio, sicome la musica, esso poeta non può descrivere l'armonia della musica, perchè non ha potestà in un medesimo tempo di dire diverse cose, come la proportionalità armonica della pittura composta di diverse membra in un medesimo tempo, la dolcezza delle quali sono giudicate in un medesimo tempo, cosi in comune, come in particolare; in comune, inquanto allo intento del composto, in particolare, inquanto allo intento de' componenti, di che si compone esso tutto; e per questo il poeta resta, inquanto alla figuratione delle cose corporee, molto indietro al pittore, e delle cose invisibili rimane indietro al musico. ma s'esso poeta toglie in prestito l'aiuto dell' altre scientie, potrà comparire alle fere come li altri mercanti portatori di diverse cose fatte da più inventori, e fa questo il poeta, quando sinpresta l'altrui scientia, come del oratore, e del filosofo, astrologho, cosmografo e simili, le quali scienze sonno in tutto separate dal poeta. adonque questo è un sensale, che gionge insieme diverse persone a fare una conclusione d'un mercato, e se tu vorai trovare il proprio ufficio del poeta, tu troverai non esser altro, che uno addunatore de cose rubate a diverse scientie con le quali egli fa un composto buggiardo, o

Also music, when setting her suave melodies in rhythmic divisions of time, composes them in her various voices. But the poet is debarred from such harmonious discrimination of voices; and although poetry like music enters through the ear to the seat of understanding, he is unable to give an equivalent of musical harmony, because it is beyond his power to say different things simultaneously as the painter does in his harmonious proportions where the component parts are made to react simultaneously and can be seen at one and the same time both together and separately;[1] together, by viewing the design of the composition as a whole, and separately, by viewing the design of its component parts. For these reasons the poet ranks far below the painter in the representation of visible things, and far below the musician in that of invisible things.

But if the poet borrows assistance from the sciences of others he may as well present himself at a fair like those traders who deal in all sorts of goods from different makes;[2] for he does the same when he borrows from the sciences of the orator, the philosopher, the astronomer, the cosmographer, and others. These sciences are quite distinct from the poet's art. Hence he resembles a trader who collects a number of people to strike a bargain; and if you inquire into the true nature of his work you will find that he does nothing but join together things stolen from other sciences[3] and with these concoct a mendacious fabrication,[4]

[1] Proportions in painting are comparable to intervals in music. The proportioned divisions of space and the differences of pitch between sounds have also this in common, that they produce their effects simultaneously; while metre in poetry is more like rhythm in music —a grouping of syllables or notes according to duration.

[2] Historical painting sometimes errs in the same direction. Compare Lessing, *Laokoon*, Materialien 20: 'The true vocation of a fine

art can only be that which she can produce without the help of another art.'

[3] Compare Quintilian, *Institutiones Oratoriae*, ii. 21. 7, where Rhetoric is spoken of as an art that wanders about and speaks on all subjects: 'eamque artem circumcurrentem vocaverunt, quod in omni materia diceret.'

[4] The accusation of being untruthful was levelled at the various Arts by different writers for diverse reasons. According to Hesiod, it was one of the privileges of the Muses to be

vuoi con più honesto dire, un composto finto, et in questa tal fintione libera esso poeta se equiparato al pittore, ch'è la più debole parte della pittura.

allowed to tell lies (*Theogony*, 27). Both Pindar (*Olympian*, I. 49 ff., *Nemean*, 7. 31 ff.) and Thucydides (*Speech of Pericles*, ii, c. 41) gracefully conceded to the poet the liberty of telling lies. Then came Plato's accusation (*Republic*, x. 598) that both Poetry and Painting were completely divorced from Truth as they imitate the apparent nature of appearances and not the real nature of real objects.

Plutarch, although a friend of Poetry, began his treatise *De audiendis poetis* as follows: 'First of all we must introduce youth to Poetry, admonishing it, however, mainly to keep in mind and in view the diction . . . poets tell many lies sometimes intentionally and sometimes unintentionally' (Ch. 2). In *Moral.* 348c Plutarch, examining the deception inherent in the art of drama, affirms that a poet who deceives is wiser than one who does not.

The following passages in Shakespeare's *Timon of Athens* (Act I) are apposite:

Apamentus: Art not a poet?

Poet: Yes.

Apamentus: Then thou liest.

Timon gives the preference to painting:

or let us call it an imaginary fabrication, to give it a more respectable name; and the poet compares such freedom of his imagination with the painter's, although this is the weakest side of Painting.[1]

'Painting is welcome.

The Painting is almost the natural man

For since dishonour traffics with man's nature

He is but outside. These pencill'd figures are

Even such as they give out. I like your work.'

For a justification of Poetry see Aristotle, *Poetics*, ix.

The sculptor Tribolo, in his letter to Benedetto Varchi (Bottari e Ticozzi, i. 27), maintained that Painting was based on make-believe and deception, as it produced the appearance of form and space on a flat surface. In fact, if he had to represent deceit he would choose the painter as its personification. Sculpture according to him was truthful, like nature, and without make-believe. Philostratus the Younger (Εἰκόνες Proœmium) says: 'The deception inherent in the (painter's) work is pleasurable and involves no reproach.'

[1] Subjects of pictures dealing with extrinsic matter constitute the most debatable aspect of the art (p. 43).

IV

PAINTING AND SCULPTURE

a. TO ADD AND TO SUBTRACT

'What is it that impresses you when you look at something, which attracts you, captivates you and fills you with joy? We are all agreed that it is the interrelation of parts towards one another and towards the whole, with the added element of beauty of colour, which constitutes beauty as perceived by the eye.'—PLOTINUS, *Ennead.*

MATHEMATICAL considerations played an important part in the debate between sculptors and painters. Alberti began his treatise on Sculpture by distinguishing systematically between the modellers who sometimes add and sometimes subtract the clay or wax in building their figures; the carvers, who proceed by subtraction only, in cutting their figures out of blocks of stone; and thirdly the silversmiths, who proceed by addition only, extending their material to the required shape.[1]

Leonardo claimed proficiency in the three techniques when he offered his services to the Duke of Milan: 'I can carry out sculpture in marble, bronze or clay'.

The quality of the artist's material determines his technique. The bronzeworker casts his fluid metal into a shaped mould. The modeller in clay starts from nothing, and proceeds to build up a figure in three dimensions. Leonardo uses the expression *crescere*, to grow, to describe the building up of a model in clay, preliminary to the casting in bronze. 'Quando tu ai finito di crescere l'uomo tu farai la statua' (R. 802). He modelled the Sforza monument in clay.

The carver, on the other hand, starts from a block wherein both the figure and the space surrounding it are potentially enclosed, and he gradually uncovers the figure by clearing the space around it.[2]

For the sake of comparison Painting was considered related to the arts which proceed by addition. According to Leonardo the sculptor's

---

[1] A similar distinction was made by classical writers. See A. J. B. Wace, *An Approach to Greek Sculpture*, 1935; Pliny, *Nat. Hist.* xxxv.

[2] Among modern sculptors Maillol was essentially a carver: 'For me sculpture means the block.' Whereas Epstein prefers the modeller's technique: 'Modelling seems to me more genuinely creative. It is the creating of something out of nothing.'

work consists in subtracting material; the painter's in continually adding material; but while the material which the sculptor removes is always of the same kind, that which the painter adds varies continually (p. 102, Trat. 39).

Alberti found that painters, when consulted, denied being chiefly concerned with the addition of material. They claimed to have a way of their own. Obviously their art was not so simple. While the sculptor working in but one material relied on nature to supply the three dimensions, the spatial environment, and the light and shade, the painter had to create all these with his colours.

G. P. Lomazzo felt that the three-dimensional substance which gave to sculpture its solidity could not be compared to the colours which the painter added to his canvas.[1] He, therefore, identified the substance of painting with 'proportional quality'. 'Painters must consider carefully that proportional quality means the same as drawing, and that drawing stands for the substance of painting' (*Trattato dell' Arte della Pittura*, I. i. 24). But drawing is practised by both sculptors and painters. If we reduce the techniques to a relationship which they share in common and confine ourselves to the processes of addition and subtraction, regardless of the material, it is evident that these were but means to establish the relative proportions of the parts to the whole. Painters and sculptors alike had to fall back upon the art of drawing, the foundation of all the visual arts.

Alberti recalls the three processes of taking off, putting on, and changing when dealing with proportions in architecture:

'The beauty of a thing depends on the adjustment of all parts in proportion, so that one cannot *add or take off, or change* anything without impairing. And this is certainly a great and divine thing after which the arts and the sciences strive with all their power, and it is rarely conceded to anyone, even to nature herself, to bring forth a work that is complete and perfect from every point of view.'

The same principles were said to obtain in literature. Quintilian (*Inst. Orat.* ix. 4. 147) recommends the use of three ways, 'De ratione in adjectione, detractione, mutatione', to stylists in the study of rhetoric

---

[1] Compare Plato's description of the painter's technique: '. . . It seems as if it would never stop laying on colours or taking them off, or whatever the professional painters term the process, to reach a point where the picture admits of no further improvement in respect of beauty and lucidity' (*Laws*, vi, 769, trans. Bury).

and literary composition. Aristotle applies the same methods to composition in poetry.

'As in the other arts of representation a single representation means a representation of a single object, so too the plot being a representation of a piece of action must represent a single piece of action and the whole of it; and the component incidents must be so arranged that if one of them be altered or removed, the unity of the whole is disturbed and destroyed. For if the presence or absence of a thing makes no visible difference, then it is not an integral part of the whole' (*Poetics* 8).

The visual and poetic arts, and Music also, are based on similar mathematical operations which aim at the adjustment of the parts to the whole in order to form a unity. This is what is impressed on the artist's mind, what he strives after, and what he imprints on the material wherewith he works.

The art of the sculptor is introduced in suggestive similes in Renaissance Literature, and is compared with the creation of man by God. Marsilio Ficino, the Florentine Platonist, in his commentary to Dionysos the Areopagite, says: 'If God made man in his own image, God's statue is certainly in man though concealed.' The Areopagite had compared the mystic perception of the supernatural, which is achieved by the shedding of all extraneous matter, to the process of the sculptor who carves away the obstructions that conceal the form of his statue (*Mystica Theologia*, c. 2).

Vasari in the introduction to the *Lives* claims the Most High as the first artist, and proceeds to describe the creation of man as the penetration by His Spirit of a solid mass of earth:

'. . . The model, therefore, from which the first image of man arose, was a mass of earth; and not without significance since the Divine Architect[1] . . . designed to instruct us by the imperfection of the material in the true method of attaining perfection, by repeatedly diminishing and adding to; as the best sculptors and painters are wont to do, for by perpetually subtracting from or adding to their models they conduct their work from its first imperfect sketch to that finish of perfection which they desire to attain.'

An amusing passage in R. Borghini's *Il Riposo* (1584) is probably based on this passage of Vasari. In a discussion on the relative merits of Painting and Sculpture the protagonist of the latter claims God as the

---

[1] Compare the description of Zeus by Kleanthes, p. 13.

first Sculptor, but is refuted because the Creator made man of earth, that is to say, of clay, and therefore could not have worked by subtracting—*per via di levare*—which is the only true kind of sculpture (ed. 1807, 134). Also Michelangelo considered stone-carving the only true sculpture. He described its progressive stages as follows: 'One must imagine the figure as if it were lying under a body of water which is allowed gradually to run off, thus permitting the figure to come little by little above the surface, until at length it lies completely exposed.' In one of Michelangelo's finest sonnets, said to have been addressed to Vittoria Colonna, the figure, potentially contained in a block of marble and waiting for the sculptor's chisel to be laid bare, is compared to qualities dormant in human nature and waiting to be brought out by love and friendship.

> The best of artists have no thought to show
> Which the rough stone in its superfluous shell
> Doth not include; to break the marble spell
> Is all the hand that serves the brain can do.
>
> (Trans. A. J. Symonds.)

b. THE PLASTIC AND PICTORIAL POINTS OF VIEW

'The painter gives on a plane a visual impression of a three-dimensional form, while the sculptor forms something three-dimensional for the purpose of affording a plane visual impression.'—ADOLF HILDEBRAND.[1]

The rivalry between the painter and the sculptor involved two contrasting aspects of the visual arts, the plastic and the pictorial, wherein the Florentine school was pitted against the Venetian. Michelangelo may be regarded as representing the Florentine ideal. Francisco de Hollanda found him severely critical of Flemish painting:

'It will appeal to certain noblemen, who have no sense of harmony. In Flanders they paint with a view to external exactness. . . . They paint stuffs and masonry, the green grass of the fields, the shadow of trees, and rivers and bridges, which they call landscapes with figures on this side and figures on that side; and all this . . . is done without reason or art, without symmetry or proportion, without skilful choice or boldness, without substance or vigour' (*Dialogos*, 1548).

Leonardo, on the other hand, while adhering to his Florentine tradition, had a more pictorial approach. His love of nature made him an

---

[1] *The Problem of Form*, English translation, 1932.

PLATE XI

Drawing of a nymph

PLATE XII

Drawing of clouds and mountains

eager student of landscape. He endeavoured to render distances and the intervening atmosphere, and to convey the effect produced by the transparency of water (pp. 100, 104, 105, Trat. 38, 40, 41). He reproached his compatriot Botticelli for neglecting this aspect.

'He who does not care for landscapes esteems them a matter involving merely cursory and simple investigations. So does our Botticelli, who says that such studies are vain, since by merely throwing a sponge soaked in different colours at a wall, a spot is formed, wherein a lovely landscape might be discerned' (Trat. 60).

In another passage Leonardo suggests using such accidental marks on a wall as Botticelli scorned as a preliminary idea for a composition. He started by visualizing his subject as a pattern on a flat surface.

'When you look at a wall spotted with stains or by a mixture of stones, if you have to devise some scene, you may discover a resemblance to various landscapes, with mountains, rivers, rocks, trees, plains, valleys and hills in varied arrangement; or again you may see battles and figures in action; or strange faces and costumes and an endless variety of objects, which you could reduce to complete and well drawn forms. And these appear on such a wall confusedly, like the sound of bells in whose jangle you may find any name or word you may choose to imagine' (R. 508).[1]

Leonardo's way of rendering form by planes rather than by outlines is inspired by the painter's point of view. His description of contours is similar to Cézanne's:

'The boundary of one thing with another is of the nature of a mathematical line, because the end of one colour is the beginning of another colour and is not to be called line . . . the boundary is a thing invisible' (Trat. 486).

'Les contrastes et les rapports des tons, voilà le secret du dessin et du modelé, car la forme et le contour des objets nous sont donnés par les oppositions et les contrastes qui resultent de leur colorations particulières' (Cézanne).

In comparing the two arts Leonardo looks at a statue as a purely visual image with the eye of a painter. He asserts that even its three-dimensional solidity can be rendered as convincingly in a picture (p. 108,

---

[1] Modern French painters like to quote this passage of Leonardo when they describe the aims and methods of Surrealism and their predilection for unexpected combinations. André Lhote does so when asserting that all sorts of objects assembled by chance are apt to inspire beautiful and unusual relationships of colours and forms. Amedée Ozenfant does so when writing of poets who draw inspiration for the wording of their verses from chance noises such as the clatter of a moving train, for instance. Visions and thoughts are superimposed on suggestive sights and sounds as weft is woven into the warp of a loom.

Trat. 45), and that therefore the painter's work is superior intellectually because he has to produce the effects of the illumination and foreshortening, while the sculptor relies on nature to supply these (pp. 94–101, Trat. 35, 36, 38, 39). But this free gift has its disadvantages. The lighting of a statue is not such a simple matter as is sometimes supposed. It involves the avoidance of distracting cast shadows, and the disposal of the illumination on the right portion. A sensitive appreciation and understanding is required to find the light for which the sculptor designed his work. A painting, on the other hand, carries its own illumination as one of its intrinsic qualities (pp. 95–101, 104–109, Trat. 36–8, 42–5).

One of the arguments in favour of Sculpture when compared to Painting was that statues could be viewed from every side. The painter had to consider only one aspect of the subject, while the sculptor had to deal with a number of views. His task was therefore more difficult and his work more complete. Cellini asserted self-confidently that Sculpture was seven times better than Painting because it does not confine itself to one view of the subject but gives eight of them.

But the sculptor has his own difficulties. He must combine these different views into one whole, though he cannot see them all together at one time. While he is carving on one side he may unwittingly chip off too much from another (p. 96, Trat. 36). He must form his statue by joining and fusing a sequence of visual images. As he works visual and tactual sensations interlink. This response to the sense of touch as well as to the sense of sight was considered a point in her favour by the protagonists of Sculpture. 'It is truer to nature, in touching it you can feel it', argues Maestro Tasso. 'A blind man by touching it responds to it', says Tribolo.[1]

Cellini relates that Michelangelo, whom he calls the greatest painter of all time, began his paintings by making carefully studied models in the round for the various figures in his compositions; and that he did likewise for his architectural designs.[1] For him the realization of the solid form came first. Leonardo, on the other hand, approaches these problems from the painter's standpoint. One of his retorts to such arguments is that the sculptor need only execute the front and the back view (pp. 98, 107, Trat. 37, 43).

---

[1] These opinions of Tasso, Tribolo, and Cellini were given in answer to Varchi's questionnaire. See p. 88.

There is a painting which seems to have some connexion with this contention, the 'David and Goliath' by Daniele da Volterra (1555). It is double-faced, the front and back views of the group being painted on either side of a sheet of slate. According to Vasari (ed. Milanesi, vii. 61) the artist was asked by the learned Giovanni della Casa, who was writing a treatise on painting, to model a figure of David in clay and then paint the front and the back view of it, a task for which he was eminently fitted as he was both sculptor and painter. He succeeded so well that after his death his work was presented to Louis XIV as a masterpiece by Michelangelo, and found its way into the Louvre.

When Leonardo asserted that the sculptor need only consider the front and back views of his figure he may have had in mind the stone-carver's initial conception of his figure as a relief; and he considered relief work more like painting than sculpture in the round (pp. 104, 107, Trat. 40, 42). Elsewhere he freely admits that the sculptor must draw numerous outlines for his work to look well on all sides (p. 95, Trat. 36). But he does not consider this an argument in his favour, since a unified effect, seen all at once from one point of view, was prerequisite (p. 68).

Another answer to the sculptor was given by Giorgione in Venice. In Paolo Pino's *Dialogo della Pittura* (Venice, 1548) the story is told how, to the utter confusion of certain sculptors, Giorgione painted a Saint George in armour standing on the banks of a limpid stream and between two mirrors reflecting the figure at various angles. The artist wished to prove that a painting could display various aspects of the same figure which could be viewed all at one glance, and without the necessity of walking round it. The story is confirmed by Vasari in his second edition (1568) written after his visit to Venice. But here the subject is described as a nude figure with armour placed on one side (ed. Milanesi, iv. 95 and i. 101). Giorgione is said to have painted the picture after a discussion which took place in front of Verocchio's bronze horse, where certain sculptors had boasted that a statue could be enjoyed from many points of view. This monument was unveiled in 1496, and Leonardo must have looked at his former master's work with intense interest during his visit three years later, comparing it with the Sforza monument which he had left unfinished at Milan. We may think of him as enjoying its different aspects, and embarking on a discussion with arguments such as appear in the *Paragone*.

Vasari's story shows that also Giorgione and his friends liked to linger in front of the same monument, which to them must have seemed the embodiment of the Florentine plastic ideal.

c. PARTICIPANTS IN THE DEBATE

Leonardo was voicing the opinion of his time when he argued as the protagonist of Painting. For this art had achieved a spectacular development and in the eyes of the people had taken the leading part which Sculpture was believed to have played in ancient times. It is indicative of the change that Leon Battista Alberti in describing the origin of Painting compares the painter to Narcissus gazing enamoured at the reflection of his face in a mountain pool; while Ovid, from whom the story is taken, compares the reflection to a head carved in Parian marble.

Leonardo's comparison of the two arts may be said to have started a debate which continued through centuries; and the questions of form, space, and colour which were involved still occupy artists of to-day.

He probably expressed his views in one of the above-mentioned 'scientific duels' which were staged at the court of Lodovico il Moro. His opponent in the debate may have been the sculptor Gian Cristoforo Romano, known to have been a singer in Beatrice d'Este's choir at that time. Among the listeners may have been Baldassare Castiglione, who spent part of his youth at Milan, where he had influential relatives. In the *Cortigiano*, that handbook of what was good form, first published in 1528, the question as to whether Painting was superior to Sculpture was put by the enlightened Signora Emilia Pia to a circle of friends, who had gathered at the court of Urbino, and was debated by the Conte Lodovico Canossa and the above-mentioned Gian Cristoforo Romano with arguments similar to Leonardo's. For these discussions were not only of interest to artists and theorists, they were also the delight of distinguished society, whose ambition it was to patronize the arts and to be immortalized by them.

Somewhat later Benedetto Varchi sent a questionnaire, probably the first of its kind in history, to a number of Florentine artists, to the sculptors Michelangelo, Tribolo, G. B. Tasso, Cellini, and to the painters Bronzino, Pontormo, Vasari, F. Sangallo. In their replies[1] dated 1546–9 each artist reveals his aims and methods while reflecting

[1] G. Bottari, S. Ticozzi, op. cit., vol. i.

the views on art of the time. The arguments are similar to those used in the *Paragone*. But Leonardo is not mentioned. There is but a disparaging reference to him in Michelangelo's reply.

Pontormo's witty vindication of painting is here given at length as it summarizes the arguments that were being bandied to and fro:

'The pleasure which I know you, Messer Benedetto, are taking in fine paintings and sculpture, and your friendship towards artists, make me think that what you have in mind is an investigation of the relative importance and scope of these arts, certainly an attractive and most difficult subject worthy of your rare genius and subtle intellect. In answer to your very kind inquiry of some days ago, I do not know or perhaps am not able to express adequately in words and in ink the difficulties of the artist. I shall therefore simply give you some arguments and examples as they occur to me, without drawing any definite conclusion. For the subject in itself is so difficult that one cannot argue about it and still less solve it.

'There is but one thing that is important, and it is fundamental. That is a knowledge of drawing. Beside this all other theories are vain. It is obvious that he who can draw excels in both arts. We should therefore either concentrate on this, beside which all other arguments are vain and trivial, or leaving it aside, embark on endless discussions which lead nowhere. For instance we may say that a piece of sculpture executed in the round and to be viewed from every side has been carved by means of chisels and other tiring tools[1] and that we cannot conceive how these tools can in certain places, pierce the hard stone and prepare its surface, a task hard to execute even in the softer medium of clay. Or we may speak of the difficulty of carving an arm raised in the air and holding something in the hand, a precarious and awkward thing to achieve without a breakage. Or we may say that if the sculptor chips off a little too much he cannot correct his mistake.[2] He may have drawn his figure perfectly from one point of view and then not be able to make the other points of view coincide, for lack of stone in some parts. For it is very difficult for him to relate the proportions of all parts to the whole, when he is never able to see them all at once from every side; and unless the adjustments to be made are very slight there is no remedy. Thus he who is not well grounded in drawing will commit errors and oversights which are too obvious; for even slight errors in these two arts are difficult to conceal.

'Then there is the question of the various techniques, according to whether the artist works in marble and the various kinds of stone, in stucco, in bronze, in clay or any other mediums, all of which require much practice, and entail

[1] Compare pp. 94, 102, Trat. 36, 39.   [2] Compare pp. 96, 107, Trat. 36, 43.

N

no small amount of physical exertion besides. But this improves a man's
health and complexion; while with the painter it is just the opposite. He is
being worn out by fatigues that are mental rather than physical.[1] For he is
too intent and anxious to imitate by means of colours all the things that
nature has created, making them look similar and even better, so as to enrich
his works with a variety of things. He supplies whatever lighting is required,
such as fires and other illuminations in night-scenes, air, clouds, distances and
foregrounds in landscapes, buildings displaying different views in perspective,[2] various kinds of animals, all in a great variety of colours and many
other things which he may at will introduce into his compositions—which
nature could never do. He can, therefore, as I said above, improve on nature
with his art by adding grace to his figures and adapting and composing them
as seems best.

'Then there is the question of the various techniques—fresco, oil, tempera
and glue, which all require much practice in order to learn how to handle
the many different colours and know the effects produced by mixing them
in so many different ways—*clair-obscur*, shadows and lights, reflections, and
numberless other qualities.[3] But, as I said, the painter is too intent to outdo
nature by imbuing a figure with spirit and with life, and creating it on a
plane surface.[4] He should at least have considered that when God created
man, He formed him in relief, as it was easier thus to put life into him, and
he would not have undertaken a task so complicated, so miraculous and
divine.

'As another example one may say that Michelangelo could not display the
depth of his design and the greatness of his divine genius in his stupendous
sculptures, but did so in his wonderful paintings with their great variety of
figures, fine action, and foreshortenings. He, therefore, preferred this more
difficult art as being better adapted to his supernatural genius, although he
knew that his eternal fame depended on sculpture, an art so noble and everlasting,[5] but for this everlasting quality sculpture is indebted to the quarries
of Carrara even more than to the skill of the artist. For it is there that the
great masters found the marble which contributed so much to the glory and
fame and to the honours that are awarded them for their skill.

'I think therefore that we may compare the two arts to clothes of different
quality; a sculpture to a fine cloth which lasts long and is expensive, and a
painting to a cloth cottoned by hell and cheap, because it is no good once the
nap is worn off. But neither will last forever, for everything comes to an
end. And there would still be many more arguments. But pray forgive me for

[1] Compare pp. 94, 102, Trat. 36, 39.   [4] Compare p. 94, 108, Trat. 35, 45.
[2] Compare pp. 100, 104, 105, Trat. 38, 40, 41.   [5] Compare pp. 97, 100, 108, Trat. 37, 38, 43.
[3] Compare pp. 100, 104, 105, Trat. 38, 40, 41.

not having the heart to make this pen go on writing. In addition to all this important information I beg to say that I am at your service and ready to give you pleasure. I am aware that my pen is now recovering its vigour and is flowing so copiously that these sheets may not be sufficient. Therefore, in order not to bore you with ceremonies, I shall only fill it with ink just enough to note the day of the month which is the 15th of February.

Your Jacomo at home.'

Michelangelo's reply to Varchi was written in Rome in 1549.

'Messer Benedetto,

So that it may be clear that I have received your booklet, which has reached me, I will say something in reply to your questions, although ignorant. It seems to me that the nearer painting approaches sculpture the better it is, and that sculpture is worse the nearer it approaches painting. Therefore, it has always seemed to me that sculpture was a lantern to painting and that the difference between them is as that between the sun and the moon. But after reading your booklet where you say that, speaking philosophically, things that have the same end in view are the same, I have changed my mind, and I now say that if the use of greater discretion and labour, and the overcoming of greater difficulties and impediments do not confer greater merit, then painting and sculpture are equal. If this be so, every painter should not fail to practise sculpture as well as painting, and similarly every sculptor painting as well as sculpture. By sculpture I mean that which is done by carving—sculpture that is done by adding on resembles painting. In short, since both Sculpture and Painting require similar accomplishments they might be induced to make peace with one another and give up these disputes, which waste more time than it takes to produce a statue. As for him[1] who wrote that painting was nobler than sculpture, if he understood the other subjects on which he wrote no better than this, my servant could have done better. I might continue indefinitely to speak on such subjects, but, as I said, it would take too much time, and I have little to spare, as I am old and almost to be counted among the dead. Therefore, please excuse me. I recommend myself to you, thanking you to the best of my abilities, for bestowing too much honour on one so undeserving.

Your Michelangelo Buonarotti in Rome.'

At the time when the letters were written the age of scientific experiments and theories had passed. The argumentations about the arts obviously seemed amusing to Pontormo and somewhat futile to Michelangelo. But the questionnaire caused much excitement in Florence.

[1] Reference to Leonardo.

The two contrasting aspects of figurative arts, the plastic as opposed to the pictorial, formed the theme of a number of treatises which appeared in Venice towards the middle of the sixteenth century. The writers delighted in introducing personal elements. Michelangelo was set against Titian or Raphael, the Florentine tradition against the Venetian. In the *Dialogo della Pittura* by Paolo Pino, mentioned above, a Florentine and a Venetian begin by visiting an assembly of twenty-five beautiful women. The Florentine maintains that beauty is to be sought in the harmony of proportions and cannot be found to perfection in one single woman; the Venetian looks for beauty in the works of nature such as they are. The art of Painting is considered greater than Sculpture, since it has more scope. The rendering of distances is thought important, and in this the Flemings are said to excel.

In the following year appeared a reply from the witty Florentine writer Antonio Francesco Doni, who in his *Dialogo del Disegno* (Venice, 1549) introduced the author of the previous publication, Paolo Pino, as his spokesman for Painting, and a Florentine sculptor as his opponent. Michelangelo's view is maintained that Sculpture is to Painting as the real object is to its shadow.

Lodovico Dolce in his *Dialogo della Pittura* (Venice, 1557) voices the views of Titian's friend and protagonist Pietro Aretino: 'Surely colour is of greater importance and power.'

Raffaele Borghini devotes the first chapter of *Il Riposo* (Florence, 1584) to the relative merits of Sculpture and Painting. We are introduced to the villa of a distinguished patron of Art where three Florentine gentlemen, among them the sculptor Ridolfo Sirigatti, meet one day in spring, and surrounded by works of art, discuss the much debated question. In the course of the argument Leon Battista Alberti and Castiglione are given as authorities in favour of Painting. The discussions were continued by succeeding generations. Federigo Zuccaro, first President of the Accademia di San Luca in Rome, founded in 1593, was determined to banish 'these fruitless quarrels' from his institution. But he could not refrain from taking sides and awarding the palm to Painting for being more directly related to the 'Disegno Interno'—the shaping of designs in the mind (*L'Idea de' Pittori, Scultori, et Architetti*, ii. 13; compare p. 21 footnote).

A century later, in 1695, Benedetto Bresciani, secretary to Gian Gaston de' Medici, wrote: 'The friendly controversy on painting and

sculpture among these gentlemen reminds me of the old and difficult problem so often discussed in private gatherings and public academies, to determine which art comes first. The two parties formed long ago still increase in number day by day.' Thus the discussion on this theme flowed on. But they did not lead to clearer realizations than Leonardo had proposed. On the contrary, the waters on leaving their deep source spread into shallower streams.

In conclusion let us quote a few verses from Théophile Gautier's poem *L'Art* where the imposition of form upon the intractable material which the poet must handle is compared to the process of stone-carving. Like the sculptor of the Renaissance he exalts works of art that entail difficulties and can resist the ravages of time; and like Leonardo he cites the process of enamelling as a way to make painting more durable. There is a longing throughout to make art outlast life, and to express eternal values in everlasting material, ideas belonging to an age which distinguished sharply between the impermanency of man and the durability of his monuments.

Oui, l'œuvre sort plus belle
D'une forme au travail
   Rebelle,
Vers, marbre, onyx, émail . . .

All things are doubly fair
If patience fashion them
   And care—
Verse, enamel, marble, gem . . .

Statuaire, repousse
L'argile que pétrit
   Le pouce
Quand flotte ailleurs l'esprit.

Sculptor, lay by the clay
On which the nerveless finger
   May linger,
Thy thoughts flown far away.

Lutte avec le carrare,
Avec le paros dur
   Et rare
Gardiens du contour pur; . . .

Keep to Carrara rare,
Struggle with Paros cold,
   That hold
The subtle line and fair . . .

Peintre, fuis l'aquarelle,
Et fixe la couleur
   Trop frêle
Au four de l'émailleur . . .

Painter, despise a hue
And tints that soon expire.
   With fire
Burn thine enamel true . . .

Tout passe.—L'art robuste
Seul a l'éternité.
   Le buste
Survit à la cité,

All things return to dust
Save beauties fashioned well
   The bust
Outlasts the citadel.

Et la médaille austère
Que trouve un laboureur
  Sous terre
Révèle un empereur.

Les dieux eux-mêmes meurent,
Mes les vers souverains
  Demeurent
Plus forts que les airains.

Sculpte, lime, cisèle;
Que ton rêve flottant
  Se scelle
Dans le bloc résistant.

Oft does the ploughman's heel
Breaking an ancient clod
  Reveal
A Caesar or a god.

The gods, too, die, alas!
But deathless and more strong
  Than brass
Remains the sovereign song.

Chisel and limn and file
Till thy vague dream imprint
  Its smile
On the unyielding flint.

(Trans. by G. Santayana)

Trat. 35]   **36**

COMINCIA DELLA SCOLTURA, ET S'ELLA È
SCIENTIA O NO

La scultura non è scientia, ma è arte meccanichissima, perchè genera sudore e faticha corporale al suo operatore, et solo basta à tale artista le semplici misure de membri e la natura delli movimenti e posati, e così in se finisce, dimostrando al occhio quel che quello è, et non dà di se alcuna admiratione al suo contemplante, come fa la pittura, che in una piana superfitie per forza di scientia dimostra le grandissime campagne con li lontani orizzonti.

HERE BEGINS 'ON SCULPTURE AND ON
WHETHER SCULPTURE IS A SCIENCE OR NOT'

Sculpture is not a science but a very mechanical art, because the sculptor has to toil under the sweat of his brow; and he need only know the measurements of the various parts and the nature of the actions and poses, and that is sufficient to complete his work which shows to the eye whatever there is and does not inspire any wonder and admiration in those who contemplate it as does painting, which shows, by means of its science, wide landscapes with distant horizons on a flat surface.

Trat. 36]   **37**

DIFFERENTIA TRA LA PITTURA E LA
SCULTURA

Tra la pittura e la scultura non trovo altra differentia, senon che lo scultore conduce le sue opere con maggior fatica di corpo, che 'l pittore, et il pittore conduce l'opere sue con maggior faticha di mente. provasi così esser vero, conciosiachè lo scultore nel fare la sua opera fa per forza di braccia e di percussione, à consumare il marmo od altra pietra

THE DIFFERENCE BETWEEN PAINTING AND
SCULPTURE

I do not find any other difference between painting and sculpture than that the sculptor's work entails greater physical effort and the painter's greater mental effort. The truth of this can be proved; for the sculptor in carving his statue out of marble or other stone wherein it is potentially contained has to take off the superfluous and excessive parts with the

superchia, che eccede la figura, che dentro a quella si rinchiude, con esercitio meccanichissimo accompagnato spesse volte da gran sudore composto di polvere e convertito in fango, con la faccia impastata e tutto infarinato di polvere di marmo, che pare un fornaio, et coperto di minute scaglie, che pare gli sia fioccato addosso; e l'abitatione imbrattata e piena di scaglie e di polvere di pietre.[1] il che tutt' al contrario aviene al pittore, parlando di pittori e scultori eccellenti, imperochè 'l pittore con grand' aggio siede dinanzi alla sua opera,[2] ben vestito e move il leuissimo penello con li vaghi colori, et ornato di vestimenti come à lui piace. e l'habbitazione sua piena di vaghe pitture e pulita. et accompagnata spesse volte di musiche,[3] o' lettori di varie e belle opere, le quali senza strepito di martelli ed altri rumori misto sono con gran piacer' udite.

Anchora lo scultore nel condurre al fine le sue opere ha da fare per ciascuna figura tonda molti dintorni, acciocchè di tal figura ne risulti gratia per tutti gli aspetti. et questi tali dintorni non son fatti, se non dalla convenientia dell' alto e basso, il quale non lo può porre con verità, se non si tira in parte, che la veda in profilo, cioè che li termini delle concavità e relievi sien veduti avere confini con l'aria, che li tocca. ma in vero questo non aggionge fatica all' artefice, considerando ch'egli, sicome il pittore, ha vera notizia di tutti li termini delle cose vedute per qualonque uerso, la qual

strength of his arms and the strokes of the hammer—a very mechanical exercise causing much perspiration which mingling with the grit turns into mud. His face is pasted and smeared all over with marble powder, making him look like a baker, and he is covered with minute chips as if emerging from a snowstorm, and his dwelling is dirty and filled with dust and chips of stone.[1]

How different the painter's lot—we are speaking of first-rate painters and sculptors—for the painter sits in front of his work at perfect ease.[2] He is well dressed and handles a light brush dipped in delightful colour. He is arrayed in the garments he fancies, and his home is clean and filled with delightful pictures, and he often enjoys the accompaniment of music[3] or the company of men of letters who read to him from various beautiful works to which he can listen with great pleasure without the interference of hammering and other noises.

Moreover, the sculptor in completing his work has to draw many outlines for each figure in the round so that the figure should look well from every aspect. And these contours are composed of protrusions and depressions flowing into one another and can only be correctly drawn when viewed from a distance whence the concavities and projections can be seen silhouetted against the surrounding atmosphere.[4] But this cannot be said to add to the difficulties of the sculptor considering that he, as well as the painter, has an accurate knowledge of all the outlines of objects from every aspect and

---

[1] Compare p. 10. Paolo Giovio reports that Michelangelo's domestic life was incredibly filthy. 'Tanti ingenii vir natura adeo agrestis ac ferus extitit, ut supra incredibiles domesticae vitae sordes. . . .'

[2] Michelangelo considered oil painting work for women and sluggards. Vasari, ed. Milanesi, v, p. 584.

[3] The following description of Leonardo's

exterior is given by the Anonimo Fiorentino: 'Era di bella persona, proportionata, gratita et bello aspetto. Portaua un pitoccho rosato, corto sino al ginocchio, che allora s'usauano i vestiti lunghj. Haveva fino al mezo in petto una bella capellaia et inanellata et ben composta.' Codice Magliabechiano, ed. Frey, p. 115.

[4] 'Sculpture is quite simply the art of depression and protuberance' (Rodin).

notizia al pittore, sicome allo scultore, sempre è in potentia. ma lo scultore, havendo da cavare, doue uol fare gli intervalli de' muscoli, e da lasciare, doue uol fare gli rilevi d'essi muscoli, non gli po generare con debita figura oltre lo hauer fatto la longhezza e larghezza loro, s'egli non si moue in traverso, piegandosi od alzandosi in modo, ch'esso vegga la vera altezza de muscoli et la vera bassezza delli loro intervalli, e questi son giudicati dallo scultore in tal sito, e per questa uia di dintorni si ricorregano, altrimente mai porrà bene li termini o' uero figure delle sue sculture. e questo tal modo dicono essere fatica di mente allo scultore, perchè non acquista altro che fatica corporale, perchè, in quanto alla mente, o uo' dire giuditio, esso non ha, se non in tal profilo a ricorreggere li dintorni delle membra, doue li muscoli sono tropo alti. e questo è il proprio ordinario delle sculture à condure à fine le opere sue; il quale ordinario è condotto dalla vera notizia di tutti li termini delle figure dei corpi per qualonque verso. dice lo scultore, che, se lui leva di superchio, che non può agiongere, com' il pittore. al quale si risponde: se la sua arte era perfetta, egli avrebbe solevato mediante la notizia delle misure quel, che bastava, e non di superchio, il quale levamento nasce dalla sua ignorantia, la quale li fa levare più o' meno, che non debbe. ma di questi non parlo, perche non sono maestri, ma guastatori di marmi. li maestri non si fidano nel giuditio del occhio, perchè sempre inganna, come prova, chi uol dividere una linea in due parti eguali à giuditio d'occhio, che spesso la sperientia l'inganna. onde per tale sospetto li buoni giudici sempre

that this knowledge is always at the disposal of both the painter and the sculptor.

The sculptor, who has to take off (from his block) when he wants to indicate the depressions between the muscles and to let stand where the muscles bulge, cannot create their right shapes beyond determining their length and width if he does not look from above and below, bowing down and raising himself in order to estimate the actual extent of the projections of the muscles and of the depressions lying between, and these he can only judge from such positions. In this way the outlines are again corrected; otherwise he could never succeed in well establishing the contours and shapes of his statues.

And this procedure is called a mental effort on the part of the sculptor, his effort being merely physical, for while drawing these profiles his mind, or rather his judgement, is only called upon to set right the outlines of the limbs wherever the muscles bulge too much. The usual and proper way for the sculptor to bring his works to completion is to proceed by an accurate study of all the outlines of the body's shapes from every side.

The sculptor says that if he takes off too much he cannot add on, like the painter. To this we reply that if he were proficient in his art, he would, with his knowledge of the required measures, have taken off just enough and not too much. His taking away is due to ignorance which makes him take off more or less than he should.

But I am not speaking of such sculptors here, for they are not masters but wasters of marble. The masters do not rely on the judgement of the eye because it errs constantly, as is proved when some one tries to divide a line into two equal parts relying only on the eye, when it will be found that impressions are often deceptive. Owing to this uncertainty artists of good judgement are always on

temeno, il che non fanno gl'ignoranti, e per questo con la notitia delle misure di ciascuna longhezza, grossezza e larghezza de' membri si ua al continuo governando, e cosi facendo, non levano più del dovere.

Il pittore ha dieci varij discorsi, con li quali esso conduce al fine le sue opere, cioè luce, tenebre, colore, corpo, figura, sito, remotione, propinquità, moto e quiete. il scultore solo ha da considerare corpo, figura, sito, moto e quiete. nelle tenebre ò luce non s'inpaccia, perchè la natura per se le genera nelle sue sculture, del colore nulla; di remotione o propinquità se ne inpaccia mezzanamente, cioè, non adopra se non la prospettiva lineale, ma non quella de' colori, che si uariano in uarie distantie dall' occhio, di colore et di notizia de' loro termini e figure. adonque ha meno discorso la scultura, e per conseguenza è di minore fatica d'ingegno, che la pittura.

their guard, which the ignorant are not, and by observing the correct measures of length, width, and depth of each limb they constantly check their work as it proceeds and do not take off more than they should.

The painter is concerned with ten different subjects in accomplishing his work, namely: light, darkness, colour, body, figure, position, distance, nearness, motion, and rest.[1] Of these the sculptor need only consider body, figure, position, motion, rest—he does not trouble about darkness and light, as nature supplies these of her own accord for his statues. Colour there is none. With regard to distance and nearness, he busies himself with them by halves, since he only uses linear perspective but not that of colour, which varies in tone and distinctness of outline and shape according to the distance from the eye. Therefore sculpture has fewer subjects to consider and consequently requires less intellectual effort than painting.

Trat. 37] 38

IL PITTORE ET SCULTORE

Dice lo scultore, la sua arte essere più degna chella pittura, conciosiachè quella è più eterna per temer meno l'umido, el foco, el caldo, el fredo, che la pittura. à costui si risponde, che questa tal cosa non fa più dignità nello scultore, perchè tal permanenza nasce dalla materia e non dall' artefice; la qual dignità po ancora essere nella pittura, dipingendo con colori di vetro sopra i mettalli, ò terra cotta, e quelli in fornace fare discorrere e poi pulire con diversi stromenti, e fare una superfitie piana e lustra, come ai nostri giorni si uede fare in diversi luoghi di Francia e d'Italia, e massime in Firenze nel parentado della Robbia, li quali hano trovato modo di condurre ogni grand'

THE PAINTER AND THE SCULPTOR

The sculptor claims that his art is nobler than painting because his works are more lasting[2] and not so liable to damage from dampness, fire, heat, and cold as paintings are. We answer him that this does not add to the merit of the sculptor because the element of permanence is due to the material and not to his art. Painting can be made as worthy of esteem by the use of glazed pigments on metal or terracotta, which are melted in a furnace and then polished with different tools to produce a smooth and shining surface, as can be seen nowadays in various places in France and Italy and specially in Florence with the family della Robbia, who have discovered a process of producing large works of all

[1] See p. 20.

[2] Compare notes, p. 90.

o

opera in pittura sopra terra cotta coperta di vetro. vero è, che questa è sottoposta alle percussioni e rotture, siccome si sia la scultura di marmo, ma non è à distruttori, come le figure di bronzo; ma di etternità si congionge colla scultura, e di bellezza la supera senza comparatione, perch' in quella si congionge le due prospettive, e nella scultura tonda non è nissuna, che non sia fatta dalla natura.

lo scultore nel fare una figura tonda fa solamente due figure, e non infinite per li infiniti aspetti, d'onde essa po essere veduta, e di queste due figure l'una è veduta dinanzi, e l'altra di dietro. e questo si prova non essere altrimente, perche, se tu fai una figura in mezzo rileuo veduta dinanzi, tu non dirai mai havere fatto più opera in dimostratione, che si faccia il pittore in una figura fatta nella medesima veduta, el simile interviene à una figura volta indietro.

Ma il basso rileuo è di più speculatione senza comparatione al tutto rileuo e s'accosta in grandezza di speculatione alquanto alla pittura, perche è obbligato alla prospettiva. e 'l tutto rileuo non s'impaccia niente in tal cognitione, perche egli adopra le semplice misure, come l'ha trovate al uiuo, e di qui, inquanto à questa parte, il pittore impara più presto la scultura, che lo scultore la pittura. ma per tornare al proposito di quel ch'è detto del basso rileuo, dico, che quello è di men fatica corporale ch'el tutto rileuo, ma assai di magiore inuestigatione, conciosiachè in quello s'ha da considerare la proportione, che han' le distantie interposte infra le prime parte de' corpi e le seconde, e dalle seconde alle terze successivamente, le quali, se da te, prospettivo, saranno considerate, tu non

kinds by painting on terracotta and covering it with glaze. It is true that these are exposed to damage from knocks and cracks, but so is sculpture in marble; and there is not the danger from destruction (by melting) to which figures in bronze are exposed. As regards permanence they compare with sculpture, but they are incomparably superior in beauty because they combine both kinds of perspective, while in sculpture in the round there is no perspective except what is supplied by nature.

For making a figure in the round the sculptor need only execute two views, one of the front and one of the back.[1] There is no need to take as many views as there are aspects, of which there are an infinite number. You can prove this because if you model the front view in *mezzo relievo*, you cannot claim to have shown more of the figure than a painter working from the same point of view; and the same happens with the back view.

But the *basso relievo* entails incomparably more mental effort than sculpture in the round and comes somewhat nearer to painting in greatness of invention, as it applies the laws of perspective, while sculpture in the round dispenses with this science altogether and simply takes its measures as it finds them on the model. And owing to this the painter learns sculpture more quickly than the sculptor does painting.

But to return to the subject of *basso relievo*, I say that it entails less physical effort than sculpture in the round, but much more investigation; for here one has to study the proportion of the distances between the parts of the figures that are in the front plane and those that are in the second plane, and between those in the second and third planes in succession, and if these things are studied by you and you have acquired profi-

[1] See p. 86.

trouarai opera nissuna in basso rileuo, che non sia piena d'errori ne' casi del più e men' rileuo, che si richiede alle parte de corpi, che sono più o men' vicini al occhio, il che mai sara alcuno errore nel tutto rileuo, perche la natura aiuta lo scultore; e per questo quel che fa di tutto rileuo, mancha di tanta dificultà.

Seguita un nimico capitale dello scultore nel tutto e nel poco rileuo delle sue cose, le quali nulla uagliono, se non hanno il lume accomodato simile a quello, dove esse furono lavorate. imperocchè s'elle hanno il lume di sotto, le loro opere parranno assai (mostruose) e massime il basso rileuo, che quasi canzella nelli opposti giuditij la sua cognitione. il che non po accadere al pittore, il quale, oltre al havere poste le membra delle sue cose, esso si è convertito nelli duoi offitij della natura, li quali sono grandissimi, e questi son le due prospettive, et il terzo di grandissimo discorso, ch'il chiaro et scuro delle ombre e dei lumi, di che lo scultore è ignorante et è aiutato dalla natura nel modo, ch'essa aiuta l'altre cose invisibili artificiose.

ciency in the laws of perspective you will not find a single work in *basso relievo* which is not full of errors as regards the depth of relief required for the various parts of the figures as they recede from the eye. These errors can never occur in sculpture in the round because nature helps the sculptor; and therefore the sculptor who works in the round has not to cope with so many difficulties.

Now we come to an arch-enemy of the sculptor. Whether his works be in the round or in relief they are worth nothing if the light on them is not arranged in a similar way to that in which they were carried out. Because if the light strikes from below they appear very distorted, most of all the *basso relievos* which become almost unrecognizable.

This cannot happen to the painter, who besides having to place the various parts of his subject in right relations to one another has to interpret two great laws of nature, namely, the two perspectives and a third very great science, namely, the chiaroscuro of shadows and lights. The sculptor is ignorant of these, and is helped by nature in the same way as she helps other objects of art that would otherwise be invisible.

Trat. 38]   **39**

COME LA SCULTURA È DI MINORE INGEGNO, CHE LA PITTURA, E MANCHANO IN LEI MOLTE PARTI NATURALI

THAT SCULPTURE IS LESS INTELLECTUAL THAN PAINTING, AND LACKS MANY CHARACTERISTICS OF NATURE

Adoperandomi io non meno in scultura che in pittura, et esercitando l'una e l'altra in un medesimo grado, mi pare con piccola imputatione poterne dare sententia, quale sia di maggiore ingegno, difficultà e perfettione l'una che l'altra. prima la scultura è sottoposta à certi lumi, cioè di sopra, e la pittura porta per tutto seco lume e ombra, e lume ed ombra è la importantia adonque della scultura. lo scultore in questo caso è ajutato dalla

As I have practised both sculpture and painting and am equally versed in both, it seems to me that without suspicion of unfairness I may pronounce an opinion as to which of the two is of greater skill, difficulty, and perfection.

In the first place, sculpture requires certain lights, namely, those from above, but a picture carries everywhere with it its own light and shade. Light and shade are therefore the important thing in sculpture; and the sculptor is aided in

natura del rileuo, ch'ella per se genera; e il pittore per accidentale arte lo fa ne lochi, dove ragionevolmente lo farebbe la natura. lo scultore non si può diversificare nelle varie nature de colori; delle cose, la pittura non mancha in parte alcuna. le prospettive delli scultori non paiono niente vere, quelle del pittore paiono a centinaja de migliaia di là dall' opera, la prospettiva aerea è lontana dall' opera, non possono figurare li corpi transparenti, non possono figurare i luminosi, non linee reflesse, non corpi lucidi, come specchi e simili cose lustranti, non nebbie, non tempi oscuri et infinite cose, che non si dicono, per non tediare. ciò, ch'ella ha, è, che le più resistente al tempo, benchè a simile resistentia la pittura fatta sopra rame grosso coperto di smalto bianco e sopra quello dipinto con colori di smalto e rimesso in foco e fatto cuocere, questa per eternità avanza la scultura. potrà dire lo scultore, che, dove fa un errore, non esserli facile il raconciarlo. questo è debbole argomento à volere provare ch'una ismemorataggine irremediabile faccia l'opera più degna. ma io dirò bene, che lo ingegno del maestro fia più difficile a racconciare, che fa simili errori, che non fia à racconciare l'opera da quello guasta.

Noi sapiamo bene, che quello, che sara pratico, non fara simili errori, anzi con buone regole andrà leuando tanto

this respect by the nature of the relief which produces them of its own accord; the painter by his art supplements this and places his light and shade where they would of necessity be placed by nature.

The sculptor cannot diversify his work by the various colours of objects; painting does not fall short in any of these particulars. Sculptors when they use perspective cannot make it in any way appear true; the painter can make it appear to extend a hundred miles into the picture. Their works have no aerial perspective whatever, they cannot represent transparent bodies, they cannot represent luminous bodies, nor reflected rays, nor lustrous bodies, as mirrors and similar polished surfaces, nor mists, nor storms, nor an infinite number of things which need not be told lest they should prove wearisome.

Where sculpture scores is in her greater power of resisting time,[1] though a picture on thick copper covered with white enamel and painted with enamel colours and put back in the fire and baked has a like power of resistance. It even surpasses sculpture in degree of permanence. The sculptor may say that if he makes a mistake it is not easy for him to repair it; it is a poor argument to try to prove that a work is nobler because oversights are irremediable; I should rather say that it will be more difficult to mend the mind of a master who commits such errors than to mend the work he has spoiled.

We know very well that an experienced sculptor will not make such mistakes; on the contrary, following sound rules he will remove so little at a time

[1] The duration of a work of art was an important consideration in certain circumstances as, for instance, if the object of a statue was the preservation of the memory of distinguished men, and the encouragement of others to emulation in the hope of securing similar honours for themselves—or, as was the case in Egypt, the continuance of some sort of life after death to counteract the jealousy of the gods, and the fate of mortality. (Compare Pomponius Gauricus, *De Sculptura*, edition 1886, p. 109, and Plinius, xxxiv. 2 (4) 9 to 4 (9) 15, xxxv. 2 (2) II.

poco per uolta, che conducerà bene la sua opera. Anchora lo scultore, se fa di terra ò ciera, puo leuare e porre,[2] et quando è terminata, con facilità si gitta di bronzo. et quest' è l'ultima operatione e la più permanente, che abbi la scultura, imperocchè quella, ch'è solo di marmo, è sottoposta alla ruina, che non è il bronzo. Adonque quella pittura fatta in rame, che si può, com' è detto della pittura, leuare e porre, a par al bronzo, che quando faceui quella di cera prima, si poteua anchora lei leuare et porre, se questa scoltura di bronzo, quella di rame e di uetro è eternissima. S'el bronzo rimane nero e bruno, questo pittura è piena di varii e vaghi colori et d'infinite varietà, della quale, com' è di sopra, s'un uolesse dire solamente della pittura fatta in tauola, di questo m'accordarei anch' io con la scultura, dicendo così: come la pittura è più bella et di più fantasia e più copiosa, è la scultura più durabile; ch'altro non ha. la scultura con poca fatica mostra quel, che la pittura pare; cosa miracolosa, a far parere palpabili le cose impalpabili, rileuate le cose piane, lontane le cose uicine! in effetto, la pittura è ornata d'infinite speculationi, che la scultura no l'adopra.

Nissuna comparatione è dallo ingegno et artificio e discorso della pittura à quello della scultura, se non della prospettiva causata dalla virtù della materia e non dallo artefice. e se lo scultore dice non poter racconciare la materia levata di superchio alla sua opera, comme po il pittore, qui si risponde, che quel che troppo leva, poco intende e non è maestro, perche se lui ha in potestà le misure, egli non levarà quel che non debbe, adonque diremo tal difetto essere dell' operatore e non della materia.

Ma la pittura è di maraviglioso artificio, tutta di sottilissima speculatione,

that he will bring his work to a good issue. Moreover, the sculptor when working in clay or wax can take off or add on, and when his model is finished it can easily be cast in bronze, and this is the last process and the most enduring form of sculpture; since that which is only of marble is liable to ruin, but not bronze. Hence painting done on copper, which like all painting may be done by taking off or adding on, resembles sculpture in bronze, for when you make the model in wax you can also take off or add on; and if sculpture in bronze is durable, this work in copper and enamel is absolutely imperishable. While bronze remains dark and brown, this painting is covered with many lovely colours in infinite variety, as has been said above; but if you would have me speak only of painting on panel, I am content to pronounce between it and sculpture, and I say that painting is more beautiful and more imaginative and more comprehensive, while sculpture is more enduring, but excels in nothing else. Sculpture shows with little labour what in painting appears a miraculous thing; to make what is intangible appear tangible, what is flat appear in relief, what is near appear distant. In fact, painting has infinite possibilities which sculpture has not.

There is no comparison between the genius, skill, and science required for painting and for sculpture, for in the latter foreshortening is caused by the nature of the material and not by the artist. And if the sculptor says that when he has taken off too much material from his work he cannot join it on again as the painter can do, we answer that if he takes off too much he knows little and is no master; because if he knows the measurements he will not take off what he should not, and we therefore blame the worker and not the material for such defects.

But painting is a marvellous art full of very subtle calculations which are totally

delle quali in tutto la scultura n'è privata per essere di brevissimo discorso.

Rispondesi allo scultore, che dice, che la sua scientia è più permanente che la pittura, che tal permanentia è virtù della materia sculta e non dello scultore, et in questa parte lo scultore non se lo debbe attribuire à sua gloria, ma lasciarla alla natura, creatrice di tale materia.

lacking in sculpture, where there is only very little science.

To the sculptor who says that his science is more permanent than painting we reply that such permanence is the merit of the material of sculpture and not of the sculptor, and that he should not claim the glory for this but leave it to nature, the creator of his material.

Trat. 39]   40

DELLO SCULTORE ET PITTORE

Lo scultore ha la sua arte di maggior fatica corporale che 'l pittore, cioè più mechanica e di minor fatica mentale,[1] cioè, che ha poco discorso rispetto alla pittura, perchè esso scultore solo leva, et il pittore sempre pone;[2] lo scultore sempre leva d'una materia medesima, et il pittore sempre pone di varie materie. lo scultore solo ricerca i lineamenti, che circondano la materia sculta, et il pittore ricerca li medesimi lineamenti et oltre à quelli ricerca ombra e lume, colore e scorto, delle quali cose la natura n'aiutta di continuo lo scultore, cioè con ombra e lume e prospettiva, le quali parti bisogna chel pittore se le acquisti per forza d'ingegno e si converta in essa natura, e lo scultore le trova del continuo fatte. et se tu dirai, gli è alcuno scultore, che intende quello, che intende il pittore, io ti rispondo, che donde lo scultore intende le parti del pittore, ch'esso è pittore, e doue esso non l'intende, ch'egli è semplice scultore. ma il dipintore ha di bisogno d'intendere sempre la scultura, cioè il naturale, che ha il rileuo, che per se

OF THE SCULPTOR AND PAINTER

The sculptor's art requires more physical exertion than the painter's, that is to say, his work is mechanical and entails less mental effort.[1] Compared with painting there is little scientific research; for the sculptor's work consists in only taking off and the painter's in always putting on.[2] The sculptor is always taking off from the same material, while the painter is always putting on a variety of materials. The sculptor gives all his attention to the lines that circumscribe the material which he is carving, and the painter studies these same lines, but he has besides to study the shade and light, the colour and the foreshortening. With respect to these the sculptor is helped throughout by nature which supplies the shade and light and the perspective. While the painter has to acquire these by dint of his ingenuity and has himself to play the part of nature, the sculptor always finds them ready made.

If you say that there are sculptors who know as much as the painter, I reply, in so far as a sculptor understands the business of the painter he is a painter, and if he does not understand he is simply a sculptor. The painter, on the other hand, must of necessity understand sculpture, for he has to deal with it in representing nature, which like sculpture is in the

[1] The idea that difficulty overcome is a sign of art appealed to people in general. Hence Castelvetro made it one of the criterions of poetry, finding that what most pleases people is the marvellous, 'La maraviglia'. (*Poetica d'Aristotele*.) Compare p. 93.

[2] Compare p. 81.

genera chiaro e scuro e scorto; e per questo molti ritornano alla natura per non essere scientiati in tale discorso d'ombre et lume e prospettiva, e per questo rettrano il naturale, perche solo tal ritrare n'ha messo in uso, senza altra scientia o discorso di natura in tal proposito. e di questi ce n'è alcuni, che per vetri od altre carte o veli trasparenti riguardano le cose fatte dalla natura, e quivi nelle superfitie delle trasparentie le profilano, et quelle con le regole delle proportionalità le circondano di profili, crescendole alcuna volta dentro a tali profili, l'occupano di chiaro e scuro, nottando il sito, la quantità e figura d'ombre et lumi. ma questo è da essere laudato in quelli, che sanno fare di fantasia appresso li effetti di natura, ma sol usano tali discorsi per levarsi alquanto di fatica e per non mancare in alcuna particula della vera imitatione di quella cosa, che con precisione si debbe fare simigliare. ma questa tale inventione è da essere vituperata in quelli, che non sanno per se ritrarre, nè discorrere con l'ingegno loro, perchè con tale pigritia sono destruttori del loro ingegno, nè mai sanno operare cosa alcuna bona senza tale ajuto. e questi sempre sono poveri e meschini d'ogni loro inventione o componimento di storie, la qual cosa è il fine di tale scientia, come a suo luogo fia dimostrato.

round and of itself engenders light and shade and foreshortening.

For this reason many who have not studied the theory of shade and light and of perspective turn to nature and copy her; they thus acquire a certain practice simply by copying without studying or analysing nature further. There are some who look at the objects of nature through glass or transparent paper or veils[1] and make tracings on the transparent surface; and they then adjust their outlines, adding on here and there to make them conform to the laws of proportion, and they introduce chiaroscuro by filling in the positions, sizes, and shapes of the shadows and lights. These practices may be praiseworthy in whoever knows how to represent effects of nature by his imagination and only resorts to them in order to save trouble and not to fail in the slightest particular in the truthful imitation of a thing whereof a precise likeness is required; but they are reprehensible in whoever cannot portray without them nor use his own mind in analyses, because through such laziness he destroys his own intelligence, and he will never be able to produce anything good without such contrivance. Men like this will always be poor and weak in imaginative work or historical composition, which is the aim of this science, as will be shown in due course.

Trat. 40]

41

COMPARATIONE DELLA PITTURA ALLA SCULTURA

La pittura è di maggiore discorso mentale e di maggior artificio e maraviglia, che la scultura, conciosia che necessità costringe la mente del pittore a trasmuttarsi nella propria mente di natura et sia interprete infra essa natura

COMPARISON BETWEEN PAINTING AND SCULPTURE

Painting requires more thought and skill and is a more marvellous art than sculpture, because the painter's mind must of necessity enter into nature's mind in order to act as an interpreter between nature and art, it must be able

[1] Such devices to facilitate the correct placing of objects on the picture plane were recommended by Leon Battista Alberti, *Della Pittura*, ii; by Lomazzo, *Trattato dell' Arte*, vi.

14 and 15, and by Dürer, *Unterweisung der Messung*, &c., who illustrated the subject by four woodcuts (Bartsch, 146-9).

e l'arte, comentando con quella le cause delle sue dimostrationi constrette dalla sua legge, et in che modo le similitudini delli obbietti circostanti al occhio concorrino con li veri simulacri alla poppilla del occhio, e infra li obbietti eguali in grandezza quale si dimostrava maggiore a esso occhio; e infra li colori eguali qual si dimostrava più ò meno oscuro ò più ò men chiaro; e infra le cose d'egual bassezza quale si dimostrerà più ò men bassa, e di quelle, che sono poste in altezza eguale, quale si dimostrerà più ò men alta; e delli obbietti eguali posti in varie distantie perchè si dimostravano men noti l'un che l'altro. e tale arte abbraccia e ristringe in se tutte le cose visibili, il che far non può la povertà della scultura, cioè: li colori di tutte le cose e loro diminutioni; questa figura le cose trasparenti e lo scultore ti mostrerà le naturali senza suo artefizio; il pittore ti mostrerà varie distantie con variamento del color de l'aria interposta fra li obbietti e l'occhio egli le nebbie, per le quali con dificultade penetrano le spetie delli obbietti, egli le pioggie, che mostrano dopo se li nuvoli con monti e valli, egli le polvere, che mostrano in se et dopo se li combattenti d'essa motori, egli li fiumi più o men densi; questa ti mostrerà li pesci scherzanti infra la superfitie d'ell' acqua et il fondo suo. egli le pulite giare con varij colori posarsi sopra le lavate arene del fondo de' fiumi circondati dalle verdeggianti herbe dentro alla superfitie de l'acqua, egli le stelle in diverse altezze sopra di noi e cose altri innumerabili effetti, alli quali la scultura non aggionge. dice lo scultore, chel basso rileuo è di specie di pittura. questo in parte si accetterebbe in quanto al dissegno, perchè partecipa di prospettiva. ma inquanto all' ombre e lumi, è falso in

to expound the causes of the manifestations of her laws, and the way in which the likenesses of the objects that surround the eye meet in the pupil of the eye transmitting the true images, it must distinguish among a number of objects of equal size, which will appear greater to the eye; among colours that are the same, which will appear darker and which lighter; among objects all placed at the same depth, which will appear lower, and of objects all placed at the same height, which will appear higher; among similar objects placed at various distances, why they appear less distinct than the others.

The art of painting includes in its domain all visible things, and sculpture with its limitations does not, namely, the colours of all things in their varying intensity and the transparency of objects. The sculptor simply shows you the shapes of natural objects without further artifice. The painter can suggest to you various distances by a change in colour produced by the atmosphere intervening between the object and the eye. He can depict mists through which the shapes of things can only be discerned with difficulty; rain with cloud-capped mountains and valleys showing through; clouds of dust whirling about the combatants who raised them; streams of varying transparency, and fishes at play between the surface of the water and its bottom; and polished pebbles of many colours deposited on the clean sand of the river bed surrounded by green plants seen underneath the water's surface. He will represent the stars at varying heights above us and innumerable other effects whereto sculpture cannot aspire.

The sculptor may claim that *basso relievo* is a kind of painting; this may be conceded in part as far as drawing is concerned because relief partakes of perspective. But as regards the shadows and lights it errs both as sculpture and as

scultura e in pittura, perche l'ombre che in esso basso rileuo sono della natura del tutto rileuo, come sono l'ombre delli scorti, che non ha la oscurità della pittura o' scultura tonda. ma quest' arte è una mistione di pittura e scultura.

painting, because the shadows of the *basso relievo* in the foreshortened parts, for instance, have not the depth of the corresponding shadows in painting or sculpture in the round. But this art is a mixture of painting and sculpture.

Trat. 41]   **42**

EQUIPARATIONE DA PITTURA A SCULTURA

Mancha la scultura della bellezza de' colori, mancha della prospettiva de' colori, mancha della prospettiva et confusione de' termini delle cose remote dall' occhio, imperocchè cosi farà cognito li termini delle cose propinque, come delle remote, non farà l'aria interposta infra l'obbietto remoto e l'occhio occupare più esso obbietto, che l'obbietto vicino, non farà i corpi lucidi e trasparenti, come le figure vellate, che mostrano la nuda carne sotto i veli a quella anteposti, non farà la minuta giarra di varij colori sotto la superfitie delle trasparenti acque.

COMPARISON BETWEEN PAINTING AND SCULPTURE

Sculpture is lacking in beauty of colour, and has to do without perspective of colour, without linear perspective, without the indistinctness of outlines of objects remote from the eye; for in sculpture there is no difference between outlines that are near and those that are remote, and the intervening atmosphere cannot be suggested by the greater envelopment of the remoter object. Sculpture cannot render the sheen or transparency of things, as, for instance, veiled figures with the flesh showing through the intervening veil, she cannot render minute pebbles of different colours underneath the surface of limpid waters.

Trat. 42]   **43**

COMPARATIONE DELLA PITTURA ALLA SCULTURA

La pittura è di maggior discorso mentale, che la scultura e di maggior artificio, conciosia chella scultura non è altro, che quel, chella pare, cioè nell' essere corpo rilevato e circondato d'aria e vestito da superfitie oscura et chiara, come sono gli altri corpi naturali; e l'artificio è condotto da due operatori, cioè dalla natura e dall' huomo, ma molto è maggiore quello della natura conciosia chè s'ella non soccorresse tale opera con ombre più o meno oscure e con li lumi più o men chiari, tale operatione sarebbe tutta d'un colore chiaro e scuro, a similitudine d'una superfitie piana. è oltra questa ui s'aggionge l'adiutorio della prospettiua.

COMPARISON BETWEEN PAINTING AND SCULPTURE

Painting requires more thought and greater artistry than sculpture, for sculpture is but what it appears to be—a body in the round, surrounded by air and covered by a dark and light surface, as are other natural objects; and this art is directed by two masters, by nature and by man. But nature's share is by far the greater of the two, since without her contribution of shadows more or less deep and of lights more or less bright the work would appear all of one tone like a plane surface, and besides, nature makes a further contribution in supplying perspective which by means

P

la quale con li suoi scorti ajuta voltare la superfitie muscolosa de' corpi a diuersi aspetti, occupando l'un muscolo l'altro con maggiore o minore occupatione. qui risponde lo scultore e dice: s'io non facessi tali muscoli, la prospettiva non megli scorterebbe. al quale si risponde, che se non fusse l'aiutto del chiaro e scuro, tu non potresti fare tali muscoli, perche tu non li potresti vedere. dice lo scultore, ch'egli è esso, che fa nascere il chiaro e lo scuro col suo levare della materia sculta. rispondesi, che non egli, ma la natura fa l'ombra, e non l'arte, e che s'egli sculpisse nelle tenebre, non vederebbe nulla, perche non v'è varietà, nè ancho nelle nebbie circondanti la materia sculta con eguale chiarezza non si vederebbe altro, che li termini della materia sculta nelli termini della nebbia, che con lei confina, e dimando a te, scultore, perche tu non conduci opere a quella perfettione in campagna circondate da uniforme lume universale de l'aria, come tu fai ad un lume particulare, che d'alto discenda alla luminatione della tua opera? et se tu fai nascere l'ombra a tuo bene placito nel levare della materia, perchè non le fai medesimamente nascere nella materia sculta al lume universale, come tu fai nel lume particulare? certo tu t'inganni, che l'è altro maestro, che fa esse ombre e lumi, al quale tu famiglio però pari la materia, dove egli imprime essi accidenti. sicchè non ti gloriare de l'altrui opere. a te sol basta le longhezze et grossezze delle membra di qualonque corpo e le loro proportioni, e questo è tua arte. il resto, ch'è il tutto, è fatto dalla natura, maggiore maestro di te. dice lo scultore, che farà di basso riheuo e che mostrerà per via di prospet-

of foreshortening helps to turn the planes of the muscles to face different directions as one muscle recedes more or less behind another.

Here the sculptor replies: if I had not first modelled these muscles, perspective could not have given these foreshortened views of them. To which we reply: without the help of light and shade you could not have modelled these muscles; for you could not even have seen them. The sculptor replies that it is he who produces the light and shade by taking off from the block in carving. The answer is: neither he nor his art but nature produces the shadows. If he worked in the dark where there is no differentiation of light and shade he would not be able to see anything. If the piece of sculpture were enveloped in a fog so that the light on it were of the same intensity all round, he would only be able to distinguish its silhouette, bounded by the fog. Let me ask you, oh sculptor, why you do not attain the same perfection in your work out-of-doors in the diffused light of the open air as you do in the concentrated light indoors which descends from above to illuminate your work? And if it were you who create shadows at will by taking off from your block, why cannot you create them on sculpture in the diffused light out of doors in the same way as in the concentrated light? You are certainly mistaken; another master is the creator of the shadows and lights on your sculptures, for whom you, but as a servant only, prepare the material on to which he impresses those accidents. Therefore, do not glory in another's work. Your work is confined to the study of lengths and widths of a body and its limbs and their proportions; your art ends there. The rest, which is everything, is done by nature and she is the greater master.

The sculptor says that he will make *basso relievo* and by means of perspective

tiva quel, che non è in atto. rispondesi, che la prospettiva è membro della pittura, e che in questo caso lo scultore si fa pittore, come s'è dimostrato dinanzi.

represent what does not actually exist. One replies that perspective is a part of painting and that in this case the sculptor turns into a painter, as was shown above.

Trat. 43]   44

ESCUSATIONE DELLO SCULTORE

Dice lo scultore, che s'esso leva più marmo, che non debbe, che non po ricorreggere il suo errore, come fa il pittore. al quale si risponde, che chi leva più, che non debbe, che non è maestro, perchè maestro si dimanda quello, che ha vera scientia della sua operatione. risponde lo scultore, che, lavorando il marmo, si scopre una rottura, che ne fu causa lei et non il maestro di tale errore. rispondesi tale scultore essere in questo caso, come quello pittore, a chi si rompe od offende la tavola, donde egli dipinge. dice lo scultore, che non pò fare una figura, che non ne faccia infinite per gl'infiniti termini, ch'hanno le quantità continue. rispondesi, che l'infiniti termini di tal figura si riducono in due mezze figure, cioè una mezza dal mezzo indietro, e l'altra mezza dal mezzo in anzi, le quali sendo ben proportionate, compongono una figura tonda e queste tali mezze, avendo li loro debiti rileui in tutte le loro parti, risponderanno per se sanz' altro magisterio tutte l'infinite figure, che tale scultore dice aver fatte, che il medesimo si pò dire a uno, che faccia un vaso al torno, perchè anchora egli po mostrare il suo vaso per infiniti aspetti.

Ma che po fare lo scultore, che li accidenti naturali al continuo non lo soccorrino in tutti i necessari et oportuni casi, il quale ajuto privato d'inganno; e questo è il chiaro et scuro, che pittori diman-

THE EXCUSE OF THE SCULPTOR

The sculptor says that if he takes off more marble than he should he cannot, like the painter, correct his mistake.[1] We reply that he who takes off more than he should is not a master, because only he deserves to be called master who has a true knowledge of his art. The sculptor answers that in working in marble a crack may make its appearance, a fault in the material for which the sculptor cannot be blamed; and we answers that in such cases the sculptor is in the same position as the painter whose panel splits or is damaged.

The sculptor says that he cannot make a figure without at the same time making an infinite number owing to the infinite number of outlines which are continuous quantities. We answer that this infinite number can be reduced to two half-figures, one of the back view and the other of the front. If these two halves are well proportioned they will together make up the figure in the round, and if all their parts are in the proper relief they will of themselves and without further work correspond to the infinite number of outlines which the sculptor says he must draw. A potter turning a vase on his wheel may make the same claim, for he also can show his vase in an infinite number of aspects.

What can the sculptor do without nature constantly coming to his aid wherever necessary and opportune? And this aid is certain and never errs. Thus the chiaroscuro which painters call

---

[1] Compare p. 89. Maillol describes these struggles: 'Even when one has acquired experience, what problems present themselves, what unpleasant surprises, what errors in calculation! In this little nude, I have not reserved enough marble for the feet; I did not make them; the figure is good all the same.'

dano lume et ombra, li quali il pittore con grandissima speculatione da se generatoli con le medesime quantità e qualità e proportioni ajutandosi che la natura senza ingegno dello scultore ajuta la scultura, e la medesima natura ajuta tale artefice con le debite diminutioni, con la qual la prospettiva per se produce naturalmente senza discorso dello scultore; la qual scientia il pittore fa bisogno che col suo ingegno s'acquisti.

Dirà lo scultore far opere più etterne, chel pittore. qui si risponde essere virtù della materia sculta, e non dello scultore, che la sculpisce, e se 'l pittore dipinge in terra cotta con vetri, essa sarà più eterna, che la scultura.

light and shade, and which they have to recreate for themselves by much study of the quantities and qualities and relations, is supplied to sculpture by nature without mental effort on the part of the sculptor. And in the same way nature helps the sculptor by showing foreshortened views which perspective produces in the natural way without any science on his part; while the painter has to acquire this science by intellectual effort.

The sculptor will say that his works are more lasting than the painter's; to which we reply that this is not his own merit but that of his material, and that if a painter paints on terracotta with glazes his work will be more lasting than sculpture.

Trat. 44]   45

DELL' OBLIGHO, CH'HA LA SCULTURA COL LUME, E NON LA PITTURA

HOW SCULPTURE IS DEPENDENT ON LIGHT AND PAINTING IS NOT

Se la scultura havrà il lume di sotto, parrà cosa mostruosa e strana; questo non accade alla pittura, che tutte le parti porta con seco.

If sculpture is illuminated from below it will seem monstrous and strange; this does not happen with paintings, as they are self-contained.

Trat. 45]   46

DIFFERENTIA, CH'È DALLA PITTURA ALLA SCULTURA

THE DIFFERENCE BETWEEN PAINTING AND SCULPTURE

La prima maraviglia, che apparisce nella pittura, è il parer spiccato dal muro od altro piano et ingannare li sottili guiditij con quella cosa, che non è divisa dalla superfitie della pariete; qui in questo caso lo scultore fa l'opere sue, che tanto paiono, quanto elle sono; e qui è la causa, che 'l pittore bisogna, che faccia l'officio della notitia nelle ombre, che sieno compagne de' lumi. allo scultore non bisogna tale scientia, perchè la natura ajutta le sue opere, com' essa fa

The first marvel shown in a picture is the appearance of being detached from the wall or other surfaces, deceiving people of subtle judgement, as there is no (real) separation from the surface of the wall. With regard to this, the sculptor produces his works so that they appear as they are. The painter for this purpose must study the science of shadows in their relation to the lights. The sculptor can do without this science because nature helps his works, as she does all other material objects, which, when the light is taken away, are all of

anchora tutte l'altre cose corporee, dalle quali tolto la luce, sonno d'un medesimo colore, e rendutole la luce, sonno di varij colori, cioè chiaro et scuro. la seconda cosa, che 'l pittore con gran discorso bisogna, che con sotile inuestigatione ponga le uere qualità e quantità dell' ombre e lumi; qui la natura per se le mette nelle opere dello scultore. la prospettiua, investigatione e inuentione sottilissima delli studij matematici, la quale per forza di linee fa parere remoto quello ch'è uicino, e grande quello ch'è piccolo. Qui la scultura è ajuttata dalla natura in questo caso e fa senza inuentione del scultore.

the same colour, and, when the light is restored, are of various colours, namely, light and dark.

The second great science required of the painter, one which entails much subtle investigation, is the placing of the shadows and lights in their true quantities and qualities. These nature places of her own accord on the works of the sculptor.[1]

(The third is) perspective, a mathematical science entailing very subtle calculation and invention, which by means of lines makes what is near appear distant, and what is small, large. Here, in this case, sculpture is helped by nature, and does without the sculptor's invention.

---

[1] Among modern sculptors Rodin described modelling in light and shadow thus: 'The artist plays so skilfully with all the resources of relief, he blends so well the boldness of light with the modesty of shadow, that his sculptures please one as much as the most charming etchings. . . . Colour is the flower of fine modelling. These qualities give to every masterpiece of the sculptor the radiant appearance of living flesh.' Maillol disagreed: 'I do not know what you mean by colour in sculpture . . . I seek light but I want it simply to rest on sculpture as it falls on a wall.'

INDEX AND BIBLIOGRAPHY